Billy B

Redesdale Roadman, Border Bard.

William "Billy" Bell   1862 - 1941

Low Byrness
Otterburn
Dec. 2nd 1916.

Dear Rob

I'm afraid you would think it quite shocking
That on Sunday night we ne'er heard you knocking
Why did'nt you kick up a duce of a din
Or raise up the latch and march boldly in,
But come down tonight if the time you can spare
And gladly I'll crop the long ends from your hair
Lather and shave you, or e'en if you will
Twist your 'tash into shape as does old Kaiser Bill
A crack we will have and even we may
Have a wee drop of 'Strunt' and our toast be "The Day"
When the Allies shall knock at the gates of Berlin
And the despot of Europe shall shake in his skin
When the white flag of Peace shall again be unfurled
And her Sceptre wave wide o'er the whole of the world
I trust that The Wife and Kids are both well
Remain Sir yours faithfully. W. Bell

Letter from William Bell to Robert Craig

Billy Bell

Redesdale Roadman, Border Bard.

His life, times and poetry

William Bell,

Susanne Ellingham

Johnny Handle

Published by The Heritage Centre, Bellingham, NE48 2DF

Printed by Robson Print, Hexham, NE46 3PU

Print book Edition   2013
ISBN 978-0-9575426-0-0

The text content of this book is also available as an e-book
ISBN   978-0-9575426-1-7

William Bell enjoyed hearing his poetry recited and sung. Please feel free to perform any of his poems or set them to music.   In return, please acknowledge Billy Bell of Byrness as the author.

Cover photographs courtesy of:

Byrness Memorial Window: Revd Dr Susan Ramsaran
Catcleugh Reservoir: Northumberland National Park Authority
Hareshaw Moors: Robert Tindall

All profits will be shared by the Heritage Centre, Bellingham; The Border Library, Old Gaol, Hexham; Byrness & Horsley Parish and the Black House, Catcleugh.

Publication of this book was supported by
the Northumberland National Park Authority

Table of Contents

The poem numbers relate to the order in which they are found in William Bell's exercise books. Some were added later on spare pages or even the cover. Most poems have a date but some could be fair copies of older poems. Spelling and grammar are unchanged. Apologies for any errors made as a result of being transcribed from handwriting to typescript (around 1968) and then to digital format (2011-12).

A second e-book will contain the rest of his poetry

Acknowledgements are due to everyone who helped to preserve the poems over the years and who helped, however indirectly, in their publication.

Special thanks to Susan Rogerson's family, John Smiddy, Celia Pattinson, Pearl Baty, Ian Roberts, Ruth Dickinson, Janet Goodridge and all the other past and present staff of the Old Gaol and Border Library, Hexham.

1 Introduction to the Poems of Billy Bell
From heart to brain and pen.

Most volumes of poetry feature a selection of the works by a particular poet. This can vary from those who have personally selected their best work, or the chosen selection of compiler and publisher. In each case it is only a partial picture of the composer and their repertoire. With the Bell poems we have a full collection of his work, however, showing the development of his creative skills.

The range is a remarkable coverage of his relationship to the environment and communities of the Borders at the start of the 20th Century. Through the poems there is an immediacy of style, as they are written primarily for his own satisfaction. Frequently they join a sequence of thoughts after a day working upon road maintenance contemplating his links with nature or people he meets along the way. There is a resolution with questions of faith, in attempts to resolve the purpose of life, finding a space for all things in the order of the world.

The metre of his rhymes shows considerable variance as he can move from elaborate phrasing in one set of verses to a crisp representation of the local vernacular in another. All of this might happen within the space of a week's compositions. There is sometimes a wild sense of humour as he muses upon mishaps and conceits both in the region and beyond, with tilts at politicians and journalists.

These poems will keep the reader interested long beyond the first appraisal, as there are many hidden depths and links to explore the record of more leisurely times on the edge of a change. Yet there is a dignified richness in these years amongst the poverty and hard work. A warmth is sensed in the links of family, community and nature. A pace of rural life can be found in these pages when one can feel the Victorian values set against the essential workings of the Border communities.

The collection is a story of the man himself, leaving spaces to ponder, as all good stories do, at his own personality, and his wonderful use of words, yet content to pursue his humble job of tending the highway. Perhaps the highway of his literature reveals an inner contentment which is a joy to share.

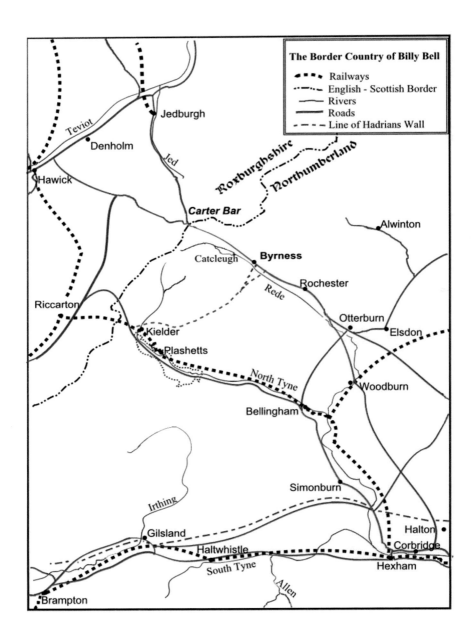

2 The life of William 'Billy' Bell

Few people today have heard of Billy Bell, the roadman poet of Redesdale, North Northumberland, who died just over 70 years ago. Only a few of his poems are known outside Redesdale - and several poems are now only attributed to Anon. This book has a selection of around a quarter of his poems. A second ebook, containing the rest of the archive, is planned.

William "Billy" Bell wrote the majority of his poems just over a century ago. He was named the "Bard of Redesdale" by local people and called "*an undiscovered poet - a poet of the mountains*" by Fred Terry, great-uncle of John Gielgud, and himself a famous actor-manager. A fuller account of that encounter is given in a newspaper article by Fred Terry (see Chapter 5) and the subsequent poem by William (*Snowbound Travellers* (336)). William Bell's subjects mainly tend to be the natural and social world around him, the landscape and people. Those people included family, friends and neighbours as well as imaginary individuals and events. The main occupation on the open moorlands then was sheep farming. Widespread afforestation only started in the 1920s. Catcleugh Reservoir was built during his watch. The church memorial plaque in Byrness gives the dates of construction as 1891 to 1904. Several of the poems refer to the people who built it and to the effect which the dam had on the valley of the Rede.

William Bell was a true son of the Borderlands. His father's family came from Northumberland and Cumberland while his mother came from southern Scotland. William himself was born just north of the Border and baptised just to the south.

William Bell, the first son of Edward and Mary Bell, was born just over the Scottish border in Riccarton, Roxburgh, although his parents' home was in Redesdale at the time. He was baptised on Sunday 6th July 1862 in Horsley Chapel, in Elsdon Parish. William Bell gave Riccarton (he wrote 'Rickerton, Roxburgh') as his place of birth in the 1911 Census. Previous censuses just stated 'Scotland' under *Place of Birth*. Riccarton, Roxburghshire, was the junction where the Border Counties Railway from Hexham joined the Edinburgh to Carlisle railway, south of Hawick. It was a very small settlement built purely for the railway workers. At this time the only easy access was by rail. The through line officially opened to passenger traffic all the way from Hexham to Scotland on 1st July 1862 although freight trains with some passenger carriages had run from 24th June. The timetable printed in the *Caledonian Mercury* in June 1862 suggests that the journey on the section of the Waverley line (as it was named later) from Hawick to Riccarton took half an hour. The train from Riccarton then took about 16 minutes to reach Kielder (which was across a moorland route from Byrness and near where Edward used to work). Bellingham, the local centre, was another half hour or so. But why would Mary be on this train? The line had been well publicised for many months before it opened. It must have seemed more attractive than the road route to Jedburgh if Mary Bell wanted to go back home for the birth. Many young wives did this with their first child at a time when rural areas seldom had easily accessible medical facilities or trained nurses. Or maybe Mary had been visiting her widowed mother and they were coming back together on the train to meet Edward at Kielder or Bellingham. It is tempting to suggest that the shaking of a train journey brought on his arrival early while they waited at Riccarton for the connecting train. Traditionally, first sons were named after the paternal grandfather but Billy was named after Mary's deceased father William which suggests her mother was involved at the birth. There were no Williams on the Bell side of the family. His brother, born 2 years later in Birness (nowadays spelt Byrness), was given his Bell grandfather's name, Nicholas.

Billy's grandfather, Nicholas Bell, son of Nicholas Bell, was born near Gilsland, Northumberland on the border with Cumberland, around 1808. He married Sarah from Lazonby in Cumberland around 1831. In the 1830s he was a farm worker just north of Corbridge at Halton Shields. His first 5 children, including Edward in 1835, were baptised at Halton Shields chapelry which came under Corbridge parish. By 1852, when his daughter Margaret was baptised, the family were living in Simonburn parish. Nicholas and Sarah later moved back to Cumberland where he was successively a labourer, a shepherd and, by 1881, a farmer of 43 acres near Gilsland. His youngest child, Margaret, was living at home with her daughter Sarah (Sallie) Bell (William's cousin) as was his London-born grandson Joseph. Margaret married William Moore in 1883 and had two more daughters. A few years later she was a widow, running Dacre House in Gilsland, with Sarah's help, as a lodging house for tourists. Billy writes affectionately to Sarah (Sallie) in two of the poems. Margaret's older brother Edward Bell had left home to work before she was born. He stayed in the Tyne Valley and in 1851 he was a shepherd for Thomas Robson at Plashetts in East Kielder. Ten years later he was working at Birness Farm in Redesdale. There was a well used route linking Kielder across the fells to Byrness and Rochester that only dropped out of common use with the advent of both the motor-car and widespread afforestation. (It is now a toll road called "Forest Drive".) He was a carter for John Robson who had 20,000 acres and employed 20 men. Mary Hope was a domestic servant in the same household.

Mary Hope first appears in the 1841 Census for Jedburgh, Roxburghshire aged 9. She is living in 74 Castlegate, and was born around 1832, the eldest child of William Hope of Jedburgh and Mary Lillie of Kelso who married in 1834. The four older children were born in Kelso and two younger ones in Jedburgh. William Hope died in 1848. The death record has a note: "Shot in the foot by accident". In 1851 her widowed mother, with 5 children at home, the youngest being 6 and 4, seems to be on parish relief and Mary is no longer living at home. However, in the same census a Mary Hope, born in Kelso in 1832, is a maid at Floors Castle. Listed at the end of 40 other servants in the household, just above the two charwomen, she could have been the scullery maid. Ten years later Mary was the senior domestic servant in the same Redesdale household as Edward and about to be married to him. This and the later censuses, as well as the age given at death, suggest Mary took two years off her age. Edward was born in 1835 so she probably did not want to appear to be older. Also, she may have preferred to claim a date of birth after rather than before her parents marriage. In Scotland her parents' marriage automatically made her birth legitimate; this was not the custom in England.

William, like his brother and a score of other local children, was listed as "scholar" in the 1871 census. Birness Chapel had been endowed in 1796 with a school for the curate to teach a dozen children. In the 1871 census the incumbent was John Nicholson, who was married with two children. In 1872 the school was reorganised as laid down in the 1870 Education Act. It had a full-time teacher and 25 pupils. William's father would seem to have been literate - and also careful with his income. When he died in 1895 his will left £214 to his wife. Some of this may have been his share of an inheritance from his father Nicholas.

Apart from a few years, around 1881, as a live-in groom on a farm a few miles south, William spent his whole life in the small cottage at Low Byrness. He enjoyed cycling and fishing in the area that used to be called the "Middle Marches" on both sides of the Borders. Many of his poems celebrate Redesdale where he lived and worked; Irthingdale and Gilsland where his paternal grandparents and cousins lived and Jedburgh and Denholm Dean which were his maternal family's area. He loved Redesdale in particular and according to Mrs Middlemas, a close neighbour in the 1930s, he used to say *"When I die my ghost will be in this valley."*

In 1881 both William and his brother Nicholas were in their teens, living and working at local farms. William, 19, was a groom at Dunnshouses, in Troughend for the Hall family. This is about 10 miles down the Rede valley, near Otterburn. His brother, 16, was a farm servant at Shittleheugh, a mile or two north. Mary Gray was 16 and a house servant in Otterburn. Around 1885 William became a roadman for the District Council which had taken over the former toll-road to Scotland in 1880. This provided him with regular paid employment for the next 48 years, his "stretch" or "length" being the eight miles south of the Border at Carter Bar. He was responsible for keeping the ditches and verges clear as well as other work when needed eg pothole filling and snow clearing. William and Mary married in 1887 and moved in with William's parents at Low Byrness (as it was increasingly spelled). The 1911 census describes it as having 3 rooms. His brother Nicholas died in 1888 aged only 23. The death certificate said he had suffered from jaundice for two years and *Phthisis pulmonalis*, ie tuberculosis, for 5 months. When Billy and Mary's son was born in 1891 he was named John Nicholas: John was for his maternal grandfather and Nicholas for both William's grandfather and brother.

Mary was a local girl. She had been born in 1864 in Elsdon to John Gray and Margaret Rogerson whose parents and grandparents had lived

6

in Ilderton near Wooler and Alwinton in the Coquet valley, respectively. These villages lie north east of upper Redesdale across the Cheviots. Their children were all born, according to the censuses, in Ilderton or Elsdon. Mary had 8 siblings. Elizabeth Gray (born 1859) married Robert Thompson in 1885. He was noted as a Northumbrian piper and a poem in his memory was written around 1910 by another piper "Kielder Jack". In 1891 they lived at a farm called Sundaysight north-west of Bellingham. Elizabeth died in 1899 leaving a son and 3 daughters. Robert, the son, was 10 and stayed with his father but the household which included Elizabeth's two younger brothers and an older brother-in-law could not look after the girls. Margaret, 7, and Hannah, 5, went to live on Tyneside with their oldest aunt, Eleanor, who had married Alexander Dunn and had a family of six children aged 5 to 20 (see *Xmas Greetings* poem No. 261). The youngest child Lillie was only three months old and she came to live with William and Mary Bell at Low Byrness.

Sadly, a few years later, in November 1902, Mary died of Acute Rheumatism and Hyperpyrexia. This is also known as "Rheumatic Fever". She was only 38. Lillie had now lost her second mother and this was the inspiration for one of Billy Bell's most affecting poems: "*Twice Motherless*" (51) . Lillie Thompson went to live with another family member. John (usually called Jack) was 11, old enough to cope in a single parent male family. The great majority of William's poems were written in the period from 1904 to 1908. William had always been interested in poetry and some poems date back to his late teens. It is reasonable to suppose that he began this intensive writing period at a time when his son would be bringing work home from school. You can imagine a companionable silence, sharing a light at the table in the downstairs room. At this age Jack would have attended the Grammar school at Hexham. This was quite a long journey by cycle and train, but he had uncles in Bellingham and Otterburn where he could have stayed mid-week in the winter, if need be. Several of William's poems show the importance he placed on literacy and a sense of duty. Working and writing together would also be teaching by example. In the 19th and early 20th century the local newspaper, the *Hexham Courant*, used to run an "Original Poetry" item. William was a regular and frequent contributor. In 1906, for example, nine poems were accepted for publication. Although only initials are given the contributor's location identifies him clearly: *W.B. Birness.*

After 1908 the poems are less frequent. If John Nicholas Bell wanted to continue his studies, and William would surely have encouraged him, he will have had to leave Redesdale. 40 years later John was reportedly working at Boots the Chemist in Swindon. Certainly by 1911 William was living on his own in Low Byrness.

Billy continued to write poetry and would extemporise verses for acquaintances, especially those he regularly met while on his road-mending duties. It was an opportunity for him to lean on his shovel and recite. Apparently he always had a stub of pencil, and a piece of paper to write lines down when inspiration struck. As he got older death appears more often. He was sometimes asked to write verses for specific occasions like hunt suppers or bereavements.

Sometime after 1911 a new schoolteacher arrived at Byrness. Catherine Ann Scott was six years younger than William and had been teaching for about 20 years, latterly in Ashington. Her family were originally from Stamfordham but had settled in Newcastle. In 1914 when he was 52 and she was 46 they married in Bellingham. She was generally known as Kathreen. She will have had to stop teaching. Married women were not allowed to hold teaching posts in the English State School system until the Second World War.

William clearly enjoyed his job - in the open air over the 8 miles up to Carter Bar at the Scottish border, usually working alone, but chatting with passers-by. *Winter on the Carter Fell* (341) describes clearing the snow with colleagues and a steam driven machine in 1917. He was scornful of the desk-bound administrators and councillors of the Glendale District who did not appreciate the hard nature of the work, described in *The Lazy County Roadmen* (361) and the resultant ills but his reaction when he had to retire in April 1933, aged 71 was

> "Sadly today I quit my tools
> One of the County's April Fools"

The *Hexham Courant* printed a photo of him on his retirement, commenting that he had a considerable local reputation as a poet.

He died in July 1941 and was buried in Byrness Churchyard, near to Mary. There is no headstone. The value of the effects left in his will to Catherine was £125. William had filled a score of notebooks with his poetry. 'Kathreen' often had them out on the table when visitors called in. Her sister came to visit her for long periods. The neighbours, who considered her "posh" and putting on airs, did not care for her. The feelings may have been mutual since she came from urban, metropolitan Newcastle and not the tight knit local rural community. She was not a fan of the poems. When Kathreen died in 1951, her sister would have burnt all the notebooks were it not for the actions of a close neighbour, Susan Rogerson, who asked if she could keep them.

Over the next 60 years there were several opportunities for the poems to become better known but it was only with the advent of modern technology that it became possible to make them widely available.

In 1960 Mrs Rogerson showed the books to a Hexham Courant reporter, Peter Robson, who wrote admiringly about them, quoting verses and saying they "had been saved by a poetry loving family". A few years later William Butler, the Director for the Northumbria Tourist Board borrowed them and had the poems typed up and sorted in the date order of the notebooks. However the chronology is not exact as some poems seem to have been written up by Billy in a fair hand but out of sequence. A copy of the poems was given to the Border Library in the Moot hall at Hexham as part of the "Butler Collection" and, around the same time, one went to the Northumberland County Record Office, now at Woodhorn.

In 1988 the "Billy Bell Project" at the Border Library tried to find out more about Billy Bell and the poems. The researcher, John Smiddy, helped by Celia Pattison, researched local registers and spoke to several people in the area, including the Middlemas and Murray families. Mrs Margaret Dunn had been one of the closest neighbours. Her father, Robert Craig, had moved to Catcleugh in 1910 when she was one and she grew up there, leaving when she was 22. Robert Craig was employed by the Waterworks Company and lived there until his death in 1948. He contributed articles to the Border Magazine and a copy of his account of changing conditions in Redesdale from 1904 to 1936 is in Chapter 6. Mrs Dunn remembered Mr Bell as her father's close friend and a good friend to her and her sister. Telegraph wires ran alongside the main road and she remembers "running a pole and walking a pole" with her sister on the way to Byrness school. Mr Bell would often measure their heights and mark his broom shank. She said he was a small man with a moustache and white hair, and, she added, he always wore clogs and would set out on the roads with a packed lunch - even after he retired. Her childhood memory of him was as "a nice quiet fellow who didn't drink or smoke". Certainly, some of his poems warn against over-indulging but there is no evidence that he was teetotal. "Lady Nicotine" also gets a mention. Many of Billy's pencils were cadged from a local farm salesman, whose son, over seventy years later, still remembers accompanying his father on his rounds in school holidays. He remembers Mrs Bell often gave him a "jammy piece" and glass of milk while the men chatted.

The Billy Bell Project research led to a short article in December 1988 in the *Newcastle Journal* about the hunt for information on Billy Bell. This prompted a maternal cousin of William Bell's son John Nicholas, to contact the researcher. John Bell, at that time married and working in Swindon had come north around 1945 for the funeral of his uncle. No further information could be found. Changes to the organisation of the Border Library and Museum in 1989 stopped further work on the archive.

In 2011 Susanne Ellingham, a volunteer at the Old Gaol, Hexham, which now houses the Border Library, began to research the Billy Bell archive further and to digitise the poems from the carbon copy typescripts. In the 1980s, before the development of computer databases, birth, marriage and death registers had been more difficult to search. She was able to find out much more about Billy Bell and his family and friends. Susan Rogerson's son gave his blessing to the idea of having the poems printed and put online. Robert Craig's granddaughter gave permission for his article to be used. Johnny Handle, who first came across the poems in the 1980s during his researches for the FARNE Archive, was enthusiastic at the prospect of helping bring them to a wider public. Support from the Heritage Centre in Bellingham, led to help in funding from the Northumberland National Park. This book is the result.

And what would Billy Bell think? I am sure he would be pleased, judging from these lines in a poem addressed to a fellow poet about the Muse of Poetry:

> TO A BROTHER POET
> ………
> Does still the charmer you inspire
> If so tis all that you require
> ………
> May she lead to the heights of fame
> And to immortality your name

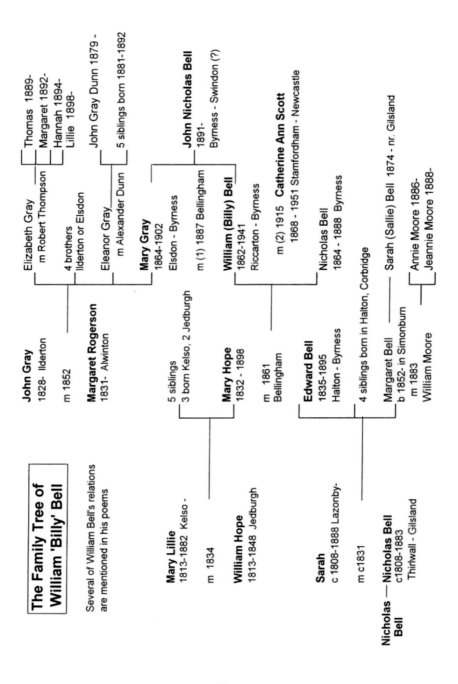

The Family Tree of
William 'Billy' Bell

Several of William Bell's relations
are mentioned in his poems

John Gray
1828- Ilderton

m 1852

Margaret Rogerson
1831- Alwinton

Elizabeth Gray
m Robert Thompson

Thomas 1889-
Margaret 1892-
Hannah 1894-
Lillie 1898-

4 brothers
Ilderton or Elsdon

Eleanor Gray

John Gray Dunn 1879 -

m Alexander Dunn

5 siblings born 1881-1892

Mary Gray
1864-1902
Elsdon - Byrness

John Nicholas Bell
1891-
Byrness - Swindon (?)

m (1) 1887 Bellingham

Mary Lillie
1813-1882 Kelso -

m 1834

William Hope
1813-1848 Jedburgh

5 siblings
3 born Kelso, 2 Jedburgh

Mary Hope
1832 - 1898

m 1861
Bellingham

William (Billy) Bell
1862-1941
Riccarton - Byrness

m (2) 1915 Catherine Ann Scott
1868 - 1951 Stamfordham - Newcastle

Nicholas Bell
1864 - 1888 Byrness

Sarah
c 1808-1888 Lazonby-

m c1831

Edward Bell
1835-1895
Halton - Byrness

4 siblings born in Halton, Corbridge

Margaret Bell
b 1852- in Simonburn

m 1883
William Moore

Sarah (Sallie) Bell 1874 - nr. Gilsland

Annie Moore 1886-
Jeannie Moore 1888-

Nicholas — Nicholas Bell
Bell   c1808-1883
            Thirlwall - Gilsland

12

3 The Comic and Dialect Poems

One of the richest and most contrasting areas of Bell's poetry is amongst his comic and dialect compositions. These vary from lengthy narrative semi- fictitious accounts of the activities of local characters to pithy humour, with an undertone of occasional morality. By reading the material in a chronological sequence, it is possible to examine his development in style as it began to increase the use of the local vernacular. The accents of the Border Region vary considerably from the softer 'Lowland Scots' to the 'Northumbrian Burr' and its more resonant use of vowel sounds. The poems often use different approaches to this according to their location. The respect for Robert Burns also had an influence on phrasing and metre in Bell's work.

The story element is produced to great effect in the three descriptions of Bellingham Show, (88, 155, 243) moving from a straightforward description for 1904 to more humorous mishaps and disasters in later years. The 1905 version has proved to be one of his best known poems. It is still performed today at rural functions and amongst the local folksong clubs and festivals. In the early 20th century the show was of great significance throughout the North, as rail transport had made stock movements much easier. In addition it was a huge social event for the farming communities of both sides of the border.

Other stories are regaled with much amusing detail such as *'The adventures of Jimmie Hastie'* (136) *'The night we spent in Coquet Water'* (153) and *'Pate's homecoming from Otterburn Ball'* (286). This comment on excessive drinking also has echoes in *'To see the King at Alnwick'* (246), where sociability inevitably ends up in a brush with the Law! *'A Baccanal's Lament'* (174) together with *'Since Geordie teuk up on the beer'* (285) follow this theme, the latter showing Tyneside Music Hall influences.

Links with Bell's work and companions reveal a detailed knowledge of rural communities and their wry comments upon colleagues, seasons, crops and the battle with weather conditions. *'The Cleugh'* (93) is an evocative roadside picture of many workers going to and from the new Redesdale Dam project. *'A crack with a collie'* (219) and *'A crack between two border shepherds'* (244) and *'Old Farmer Brown'* (250) reveal a close observation of the farming wit, at times very dry. *'The Dosin' of the Hoggs'* (302) is almost incomprehensible to an urban audience, yet this has proved to be so popular to country audiences that is has now acquired a melody. It deals with the pros and cons of an unusual potion to protect sheep from ailments.

Watching the onset of motorised transport must have been painful for Bell as his stretch of road, carefully tended for the use of more gentle horse drawn transport was suddenly subjected to attack by speeding monsters. He offers his opinions succinctly in *'Fancy Motor Cars'* (100) *'Modern Juggernaut Cars'* (148) and even gets a dig at a 'motor car driver' in Bellingham Show, likening the vehicle to a fried chip machine!

Although much of his material about fly fishing comes into the more lyrical sections of the collection, he shows some humorous sympathy with freer access to the water in *'Tammy Heslop's musings'* (251). We get an inkling of influences of other poets in the parodies *'Whist on the hunt after the wolf'* (94) based on Longfellow's 'Excelsior', and *'An up-to-date Locinvar'* (252) from the poem 'Young Lochinvar' by Sir Walter Scott. He also answered the scurrilous lines of the Hexham Poet, Chatt, forty years earlier, with his own more complimentary version of *'Hev' ye ever been at Elsdon'* (319)

Sometimes the ideas occur in a few simple verses which are complete in their economy such as *'Santa Claus'* (184), *'A little Girl's trip to London'* (187) *'Torments of Sciatica'* (276) and *'Retirement Couplet'* (355). Perhaps his late composition *'The Lazy County Roadmen'* (361) was produced only after his retirement to avoid the displeasure of the authorities.

These amusing pieces give us an insight into Bell laughing at and with himself in those remote Border hills; when listening to the poems being performed it is possible to hear from his words the music in the fine dialect speech patterns.

4 The Poems of William "Billy Bell"

7 June 1904

REDEWATERS FAREWELL TO THE NAVVIES

Farewell dear brethren of the pick and shovel
We now must bid you all adieu
For many a year you've toiled amongst us
And we wish good luck to you
We shall miss you, there's no doubting
We shall now quite lonely feel
And oft wonder what has happened
When silence again, shall o'er us steal.

When first we heard of your invasion
Twas said we'll have rough times
The navvies will the valley take
But no one now repines
We know that you are harmless men
'Though not from follies free
But then where is the perfect man
He's a mortal rare to see.

You've not molested any man
That lives up in this vale
And always been quite courteous
To all within the dale
Any little bit disturbance
Has been amongst yourselves
When you were bent upon a spree
Or held your high revels.

You will leave behind you comrades
In the old churchyard to sleep
And your little babes and children
Oft of them you'll think and weep

Beneath the old tree resting
When you are far away
They will keep on in their slumbers
Till the great 'wakening day.

You have built yourselves a monument
Which needs no sculptured scroll
Which shall stand the teeth of time
As the centuries onward roll
And to our children's children
The story shall be told
How well the Navvies built the dam
In the good days of old.

34   *4 July 1904*

ROBY'S FAREWELL TO HIS OLD MARE

Goodbye my good and faithful friend you are at last at rest
No more with me thou'll toil and work, nor sorrow fill thy breast
Beneath the waving emerald grass thou sleeps thy last long sleep
While I am left to toil alone, the wolf to backward keep.

Thou wert a willing horse to me nor'eer did shun thy work
No evil passions ruled thy life, nor in thy breast did lurk
Thou always proved thyself to me a good and faithful beast
Nor ever did the thought spring up within thy mind to reest.

Thou always pulled a heavy load, nor on the road did dally
It mattered not in Reed or Jed or any other valley
The horses they were few and far, that could keep up thy pace
Another such I'll never get to fill thy vacant place.

Not for any length of time at one job did we settle
But often shifted here and there, carting hard road metal
Upon the Carter's stormy hill we worked for many a day
And yon lead from the Ramshope burn old friend it was no play

Thou knows that I did feed thee well when from our work returning
And thy breakfast, always thou didst get in good time in the morning
Upon the best of hay and corn, and crushed beans thou wert fed
And always on to sleep at night thou hadst the softest bed.

I always did the best I could when the harness did thee nip
And well thou knows upon thy back I never laid a whip
I always kept the best of shoes I could upon thy feet
And often to thy mouth I gave the welcome looked for sweet.

Thou knows that in thy latter days I tried thy strength to save
But Ah it was the slippery roads that sent thee to thy grave
From yon hard fall upon the ice thou never did recover
No cure for thy ills and hurts, could human man discover.

At last the fates gave their decree thy working days were o'er
That thou and I for time to come should part to meet no more
My heart was grieved to say farewell, for much I thought of thee
But thou and I we must bow down unto the powers that be.

But firmly I made up my mind by Briggs thou'd not be shot
Lest for his dogs he wanted thee to boil within his pot
That ne'er a knife should pierce thee through to rack off thy poor skin
For O to mutilate thee dead I'm sure would been a sin.

Nor did I stay thy grave to dig but left that morning early
And committed that distasteful task unto my good son Charlie ,
When back again I did return, the tragedy was over
Upon thy narrow bed of clay my lingering thoughts did hover,

Farewell then good and faithful beast I soon shall be like thee
From all the toils and cares of life, grim death shall set me free
Yet onward to the journeys end I still must steer my course
But death by mighty Heavens decree comes to both man and horse.

FISHING SONG (1)

The winds from the west the soft mild breezes blow
Gone now hath bleak winter with its cold frost and snow
So we'll hunt out our tackle our rod and our reel
Again feel the joys which true fishermen feel.

We'll off to the streams where the finny tribe glide
To the sweet smiling streams of the Border the pride
Whose rippling music shall sound in our ear
As onward and upward our course we shall steer.

Away 'mong the hills dressed in purple and green
Where the wild woodlands wave in their emerald sheen ..
Where the glad birds are singing their sweet melodies
And the heather is culled by the busy brown bees.

Where the scented thyme blooms and the blaeberries grow
Where the sweet floral gems peep the green banks below
Where the moor birds are calling on each bank and hill
And the martins are sweeping the breast of the rill.

To the streams where sweet freedom still onward doth flow
Across their fair bosoms, our casts we will throw.
The bright speckled beauties again we'll see rise
Again feel the thrill as we draw in each prize.

With Greenwall, red spider and famed woodcock wing
One by one the weight to our shoulder they'll bring
From pool and from stream, behind bank and grey stone
We know to an inch, where a trout has his home.

What more better sport can a mortal require
To a fisherman true tis his whole hearts desire
With good rod and tackle and heart free from care
We'll off to the Border streams clear, bright and fair.

THE VIEW FROM CARTER FELL

Where proudly stands the Carter
In its height majestic grand
How sweet to view the beauties
Of our glorious Borderland.

What expanse of wondrous landscape
To the vision here disclose
The mountains, plains and woodlands
Of the Thistle and the Rose.

The view revealed by England
Is of wild and rugged mein
With purple heath clad mountains
And hills of emerald green.

The pastoral vale of Reedsdale
Where Reed winds on its way
Like a monster serpent creeping
In the suns translucent ray.

The steep hills of the Coquet
To the eastward show their forms
The hills, where blow their fiercest
The angry winters storms.

To the Northward stands great Cheviot
King of all the Border Hills
Down from whose rugged fastness
Flow happy wandering rills.

The view of bonnie Scotland
Is a fairy land of dreams
Of mountains, fertile meadows
Green woods and crystal streams.

Northwestward on the vision
Your eyesight will you lead
To view the charming valley
Of the clear and silvery Tweed

Yon see the rounded Eildons
Their heads in might disclose
While nestling at their bases
Lies famed and fair Melrose.

In the distant dim horizon
In giddy height there towers
The wild romantic mountains
Of the lonely Lammer Moors.

In the nearer distance lying
With its many busy mills
Reigns the Queen of all the Borders
Old Hawick among the hills.

The lovely vale of Teviot
Traversed by many rills
The Minto rocks stupendous
And the neighbouring Minto Hills.

And there where Redes clear waters
Flow o'er their channely bed
Rough Ruberslaws high mountain
Rears up its rocky head.

Then wandering from the Carter
'Neath trees and by rocks red
Flows on in glorious beauty
The lovely Sylvan Jed.

A glorious wondrous vision
Of happy fairyland
Old Jethart nestling; snugly
By its enchanting strand.

Conical high mountains
Meandering happy streams
Inspiring rocks and woodlands
Where romance ever teems.

Lovely wondrous landscape
Mans pen will ever fail
To tell thy glorious grandeur
In story, song or tale.

49   *20 Aug 1904*

NOW THE YELLOW CORN IS WAVING

Now the yellow corn is waving
Ready for the reapers hook
Golden grain and bearded barley
By the autumn winds are shook.

Bounteous plenty smiles benignful
Through the valleys and the plains
Showering blessings welcome blessings
Let us sing our glad refrains.

Now the silver moon is beaming
Courtly Queen of harvest night
Casting round her glad translucence
Shining in her splendour bright.

Now the reapers voice is sounding
In the treasure laden fields
Cutting down the laughing plenty
Which their bounty freely yields.

Soon the harvest will be garnered
Soon the autumn days be past

Soon will winter be upon us
With its bleak and icy blast.

Let us sing our songs of praises
Thanking God for blessings given
Bending Angels waft them upwards
Through the golden gates of Heaven.

50   *20 Aug 1904*

TO THE COLLIE IN TOWN, REARED ON THE HILLS

Are you not happy in your mansion home
On your carpet bed in the city
Why look around, with such sad dull eyes
An object of woe and pity
Are you thinking still of your bed of hay
Away in the hillside byre
Where you slept so sound in the days gone by
When hard work your feet did tire.

Why do you whine, and unrestful seem
And why do you start in your sleep
Are you dreaming now of the happy days
When you haulded the blackfaced sheep
Or is it of the lambing time
When you tended the bleating lambs
And why are you sharply barking now
Are you facing the horned old rams.

Or is it around the clipping bought
Along with Tip, Fan and Nell
You are housing again the timid sheep
Brought in from Blackblakehope Fell
You were happier then in these past gone days
While you roamed o'er the heathy mountain

When you rolled yourself in the heather bright
And lapped from the gurgling fountain.

What brought you away from your mountain home
Among the hills and the heather
Where in freedom sweet ran your nimble feet
In summer and winters weather
Go back again to your native heath
To follow the craft of your order
To tend the sheep on the rugged steep
Amid the hills of the Border.

51   *2 Sept 1904*

TWICE MOTHERLESS

Six years old, flaxen hair, rosy cheeks and laughing eyes
Little damsel pert and happy, you would never this surmise
That this little dainty maiden, bubbling o'er with happiness
In the few years of her lifetime, had been twice left motherless.

Yet so it is, she never knew her who brought her to the world
For three months after birth to her mother Heavens glories were
unfurled
She left behind her babe who never knew her fond caress
To a sister's care she left the tiny, little motherless.

She took it to her arms and to her heart and watched its tiny baby days
Loved it with a fond endearment smiled at all its taking ways
And fondled it with many a tender loved caress
And became a second mother to the motherless.

As time passed on the little limbs grew strong, the little feet could walk
And what maternal joys were hers when it began to talk
When first its tender lips the fond name could express
When mother, fell, from the lips of the little motherless.

She was the light and joy of home this pleasing fair haired child
Her loving little ways the sweet hours past beguiled
Four years flew past and then, O how shall I the words express
The reaper bared his hook, again, the child was motherless.

Now with kind friends she lives, but still in her young mind
Are pleasant memories, of a mother good and kind
I looked upon the child nor could I the tears suppress
To think that one so young had been twice left motherless

60   *24 Sept 1904*

NOW THE HILLS ARE CROWNED WITH GLORY

Now the hills are crowned with glory
Clothed with fairest heather bright
Magnificent their purple splendour
Bathed in noontide sunbeams light.

Now the bee flies to the uplands
Gathering in their nectar sweet
Luscious honey sweet and golden
To the place of their retreat.

Now the guns are heard resounding
O'er the heathy mountains high
Sable cock and spreckled moorhen
In the fearful carnage lie.

Why should man thus be so ruthless
This is surely cruel sport
Driving harmless birds to slaughter
Or with pain to them contort.

God made them, they are His Creation
Small units of His wondrous plan
Sent to fulfil His own good purpose
Not for sport to cruel man.

24

THOUGHTS BENEATH AN OLD TREE

Upon the hillside stands an old tree
Clothed in a dress of deepest emerald green
I paused beneath it to contemplate
Upon the years and changes it hath seen.

It is the last of a great forest
Which grew there in the days of yore
And though still clad in waving foliage
Its great trunk is rotten at the core.

I asked myself these many questions
As I stood beneath its welcome shade
How many summers hath this old tree blossomed
How often hath cold winter seen it fade.

How often have the cold winds swept around it
And shrieked their loudest in the winters gale
How often have the showers beat fierce upon it
In Autumn rains, and summers pelting hail.

How often hath it seen the summers morning
Born bright with cheeks of pinkest rosy hue
How often have its green leaves glistened
Bespatched with shining drops of pearly dew.

How often have the vivid lightnings
Above its branches, cast their lurid glance
How often with the thunders fearful peeling
Hath it felt the mountains trembling dance.

How often have the wild wolves howled around it
And the dun deer lain beneath its shade
How often hath it sheltered mid its branches
The bird on which the sweeping falcon would have preyed.

How many songsters in the prime of morning
Have there sung their sweet melting strains
In praise of Phoebus first born blushes
As they spread o'er the hill tops and the plains.

How many winters snows have lain upon it
And clothed it in a dress of spotless white
How many ages have the bright stars glistened
Above its giddy top by sable night.

How many moons have reigned above it
High up there in the deep blue vaulted sky
How many years have run their courses
Since it saw its last companion die.

The thought then came to my musing fancies
How like this old tree is to thee
Thou too art left alone without companions
That once formed thy own loved family.

The winds of adversity have swept around thee
And tossed thee with their troubled blast
Yet hopes bright sunshine shone again upon thee
And thou trusted that thy cares at last were past.

God's blessed dew from Heaven hath fallen o'er thee
Bespatching thee with blessings from above
And when His mighty voice in thunder rumbled
'Twas but to more remind thee of His love.

The wild wolves of despair have howled around thee
And on sweeping wings hath doubt assailed
Yet mid the sheltering branches of thy Vine Tree
Thy place of safety cannot be assailed.

And as the songbirds after hours of darkness
To Sol's sweet beams do all their praise express
So may thou with glad heart thus render
Praises to the Sun of Righteousness.

And though the snowy age of dying winter
May not clothe thy head with hoary hair
Yet a spotless robe of white awaits the faithful
In unknown regions, bright and fair.

And as the moon and stars oft have bespangled
And crowned the tree throughout the peaceful night
So say thy head be crowned in realms of glory
With precious gems of lustre, shining bright.

I passed out beneath its leafy awning
And traced my footsteps o'er the green grassy lea
But these are some of the many thoughts and lessons
This old tree then gave to me.

69   *No date*

WINTER (1)

Cold blows the wind o'er the northern hills
And bleak and dreary its breath
Covered with ice are the rivers and rills
Summer blooms now all slumber in death.

In a winding sheet of pure white snow
Dead Nature now taketh her sleep
The flowers and the leaves are buried below
Whilst o'er them the naked trees weep.

The drifting snow driven by the cold wind
Fills the air and hills and dales
Winter reigns with its rigour unconfined
Naught its mighty sway curtails.

The stars shine clear in the frosty night
Their virgils constant keeping
Up in the silent azure height
Whilst we mortals all are sleeping.

King Vulcan reigns in the cot and hall
And welcome and bright his sway
Giving warmth within their cosy walls
Throughout the long night and day.

On the lake the skater glides along
There delighting in his skill
While the robin sings his plaintive song
As the sunbeams slant the hill.

The shepherd on the steep mountain side
Tends carefully to his sheep
Near the sheltering fold at eventide
They their place of refuge keep.

Though beautiful and white is the pearly snow
It hath no great charms for me
I long again for the Springs bright glow
And the dewy daisied lea.

73   *15 Nov 1904*

A FOX HUNT

Athwart the fell in leaps and bounds
In full cry come the brave foxhounds
And gloriously their music sounds
As on they rush
Bold reynard trying all he knows
To save his brush.

High on the heights of Carter Fell
Amid the heath and heather bell
He thought in safety long to dwell
But that bright morn
From slumber he was rudely woke
By Robson's horn.

His course he steers by Chattlehope Spout
The scene of many a hunting bout
On to the Kirk he has no doubt
He'll safety find
But there a rousing tally ho
Quite changed his mind.

Then o'er the hill towards the Rede
Both fast and furious was the speed
Twas here old reynard did take heed
As on he flew
To try and reach the Acres high
Which well he knew.

Up on the hill above Catcleugh
He thought that he'd had quite enough
The climb he found both long and tough
So round did turn
And made the pace both hard and hot
By Ramshope Burn.

The dogs now gained upon their prey
Such furious pace he could not stay
Yet gamely he kept on his way
Up through the glen
While nearer to his fated brush
Drew dogs and men.

By Lumsden Hill so high and steep
He ran among some fleecy sheep
Which back the chasing dogs did keep

And spoiled the scent
While reynard still kept on his way
Out o'er the bent.

Again at last they struck the foil
And onward now without recoil
With naught the chase to further spoil
They raced along
And up towards the mountains crest
Went well and strong.

Their quarry on they still pursue
They now are running in full view
With every muscle strained anew
And music grand
Whose inspiring sound doth fill with fire
The hunting band.

Poor foxy still kept on his best
While nearer yet the dogs on pressed
They never thought to stay or rest
But tried the more
To win the honours of the day
And roll him o'er.

With many a double bend and turn
Now o'er the hill for White Lee Burn
O'er rocks and through decaying fern
Well, well he tried
To save his life but these brave dogs
Wont be denied.

But now his end was very near
Although to him life still was dear
Close by the rippling burn so clear
They rolled him o'er
And to this world he closed his eyes
Forever more.

THE BAGPIPER

O weird and wild was the sound I heard
In the valley far below
Where the piper piped his stirring strains
As he marched to and fro
Clad in his kilt and tartan plaid
O witching wild were the themes he played.

They spoke of the hills of his Highland home
They told of his country's glory
Of battles won of bold deeds done
Which live in laurelled story
Of the glittering stream and the flowery glade
O witching wild were the themes he played.

The wild lament in its wailing strains
Told many a tale of sorrow
Marked deep on blackest history's page
By times uneven furrow
Of treachery and friends betrayed
O witching wild were the themes he played.

From door to door he makes his way
Far from his Highland home
With his treasured pipes slung o'er his arm
A wanderer he doth roam
In the evening's hour as the light did fade
O witching wild were the themes he played.

THE ADVENTURES OF THREE WOODBURN CYCLISTS

Three famous cyclists of the North
To Hexham town all sallied forth
To see the wondrous Great Wild West
From regions o'er the oceans crest.
The shooting feats of Buffalo Bill
Did each of them with wonder fill
His marvellous powers of horsemanship
They looked upon with parted lip.
At the Cossack they in wonder gazed
And at the Indian stood amazed
The little Jap, they much admired
But what these worthies most inspired
Was the cowboy cyclist's daring leap
Which they did all in raptures greet
As mounted on his good machine
He cleared the space the boards between.
They each resolved within their mind
No longer they would be confined
To racing on a cinder track
Which of excitement much did lack
But they would try to imitate
The feats of Cody's cyclist great.
So after the great show was o'er
They faced the northern hills once more
The busy haunts of men did spurn
For their own homes in sweet Woodburn.

These three friends, named A, B, and C,
All laughed and shouted in their glee
As they sped o'er the Watling Street
Where A resolved to try the feat
Which they had lately seen performed
But the cowboy's arrangements all he scorned
The road to towering heights doth go
Then dips again far down below

Then up again doth quickly soar
To heights still higher than before
So A resolved his aerial flight
Should clear the space from height to height
He gripped his handle bars amain
Did every nerve and muscle strain
And pedalled hard with all his might
And then he took his wondrous flight
But not as A anticipated
For friends the truth must be related
Not far through space, did poor A fly
I will not reason, how or why.
He started well and quick he flew
But to an end quick his flight drew
And badly his poor face did maul
In contact with the roadside wall.
He spoiled his beauty sad the thought
But fame it is not easily bought
Now o'er the price poor A doth sigh
And says he ever more will try
To keep the fancy from his breast
To imitate the Great Wild West.

Not taking warning by A's fate
B still resolved to imitate
The wonders he had seen at Hexham
But where to try it sore perplexed him
But passing o'er wild Blaxter Moor
The thought came to him that there sure
He should not suffer dire defeat
But far surpass the cowboy's feat.
The road runs on in sweeps and bends
And onward ever onward wends
B was descending from the height
And rushing on in glad delight
But to cut off a good half mile
His fancy did him quick beguile
To emulate the cowboy's leap
Across the rugged mountain steep.

Upon the road an old cow stood
Which he took as an omen good
Ah well thought he that Yankee elf
Learned yon trick on a cow himself.
No doubt, that's how he gained his name
And also how he won his fame
So he resolved to steer his course
Be it for better or for worse
Above the heathy mountain track
By springing from the old cows back.
Old crummie stood firm as a rock
Well braced to stay the coming shock
She raised her back well in the air
As poor B struck her fair and square
Majestically he soared on high
Towards the bright blue summers sky
The glorious view he then obtained
By mans pen ne'er can be explained
He saw the valleys of the Rede,
The Tyne, the Coquet and the Tweed
Beneath his gaze he saw unfurled
The splendours of the lower world
He saw them in one fleeting glance
Then shot below, like avalanche
No more this world would have seen B
But for the laws of gravity
Once more he proved Sir Isaac right
As he descended from the height
The upward and the downward flight
Were wild sensations of delight.

But afterwards as B explained
It was the sudden stop which pained
And what surprised him friends the most
Of stars he saw a mighty host
He thought that he had gone astray
And landed in the Milky Way
Some time he lay in wonder mazed
Then up he sat and round him gazed

The scene grew more familiar now
The winding road, and that dear cow
She looked on B with mild brown eyes
While leisurely she switched the flies
Which did her fat sleek form assail
By circling round her useful tail.
Poor B's machine lay badly smashed
And through his mind the thought then flashed
That he was silly e'er to try
Across wild Blaxter Moor to fly.

However with an effort great
He made for Woodburn village straight
With face and clothes both torn and gory
Crestfallen, sad and fled his glory
Now B declares with all his might
No more he'll try the aerial flight.

Twas on the racing track that C
His bosom filled with rivalry
Made up his mind to emulate
The tricks of Cody's cyclist great
He knew that A and B had failed
Yet why should his fame be curtailed
No. They had failed in privacy
But he would let the public see
That still within the vale of Rede
Were men of action and of deed
The racing track will not be named
In case C should be somewhat pained
No chance had he to win the race
Or even gain a second place
But C conceived within his mind
As he was riding up behind
A plan by which he hoped success
Would crown his efforts more or less.

If only he could jump a lap
And land again without mishap

He knew that he the race could win
And more, for by that single spin
He would the cowboy's record beat
And gain a name and fame complete
But as Great Robbie Burns did say
And still 'tis true in this our day
The schemes of mice and men, we see
Gang often very far agley
And so it was with poor C's scheme
It ended like a broken dream
The dream was sweet when it was cast
But gall and bitterness at last
C took the leap as he projected
But landed not where he expected
The truth I must tell you, alas!
He landed prone upon the grass
Across the field he rolled amain
Then suddenly lay still again
Then shook his head and slowly rose
His efforts now brought to a close
No more he says he will compete
For honours in the cowboys feat.
O, Woodburn village, long may thou
Win honoured laurels to thy brow
Long may thy sons in manly sport
The fickle smile of fortune court
Success their every effort crown
And gain for thee and them renown.

84   *28 Aug 1904*

BONNIE JEAN O MERVINSLAW

Young Tam, went to the Jethert Games
'Twas there his fancy did befa'
Upon the charms o' bonnie Jean
The pride and flower o' Mervinslaw.

Tam winked at her, she blushed and smiled
A tryst they made between them twa
That Tam should set her hame that night
To her mammy's hoose at Mervinslaw.

Wie beating heart Tam set her hame
Encircling her waist sae sma'
And mony a kiss the rascal stole
Between Jethert and fair Mervinslaw.

Wie plighted vow to meet again
Tam tore himself from her awa'
But promised soon to come again
To see his Jean at Mervinslaw,

Now ilka Sunday afternoon
Tam dresses up himself sae braw
And climbs the Carter's stormy hill
To meet wie Jean o' Mervinslaw

Beneath the hazels leafy shade
Or by the fragrant birchen shaw
There in his arms, Tam holds the charms
Of bonnie Jean o' Mervinslaw.

Wie plighted troth and holy oath
Tam sweers that what shall e'er befa'
True unto death, he'll always be
To bonnie Jean o' Mervinslaw.

Cauld winters coming on again
Wie biting frost and drifting snaw
But snugly Tam will cuddle in
Wie bonnie Jean o' Mervinslaw.

And when the wedding day comes aff
Wie mony a hearty hip hurrah
We'll drink the health o' canny Tam
And bonnie Jean o' Mervinslaw

BELLINGHAM SHOW 1904

A thick veil of mist, the Tyne valley did fill
As I crested the top of the high Hareshaw hill,
I heard musical strains in the vale far below
As onward I pedalled to Bellingham Show.

I kept passing great crowds as I sped on my way
Smart bonnie young lassies, all dressed neat and gay
With a smile on their faces, for well did they know
They'd meet with their Johnys at Bellingham Show

An in from the mountains each valley and glen
Came the pride of the Borders, fine strapping young men
All jumping with glee, full of dash fun and go
Making haste to be in at Bellingham Show

As up through the town my old bike I did drive
The crowd was as thick as brown bees round a hive,
The rich and the poor, the high, great and low
Had come for enjoyment at Bellingham Show.

They were there from the banks of the Tyne and the Rede
The Coquet and Wansbeck and clear silvery Tweed,
From North, East, South and West, where Sol dips his glow
To see all the sights of the Bellingham Show

So up to the showyard I went with the crowd
The white sheep were bleating, the dogs barking loud
The judges were busy, they'd a tough job I know
To give satisfaction at Bellingham Show

Then round by the pens I now took a good look
To mark all the winners in my catalogue book
Appended you'll find in the verses below
Some of the exhibits found at the Bellingham Show.

There were horses and cattle, bulls, stirks, calves and cows
There was old tups and gimmers, young dinmonts and yowes,
They were there from the uplands and lands lying low.
The flower of the Cheviots at Bellingham Show.

There were dogs of all classes, both red and white cakes
There were cats, cocks and hens, chickens, white ducks and drakes,
There were pigs and salt butter, unsalted also
Pigeons, vegetables and hen eggs at Bellingham Show

The judges were called on, their approval to fix
On a fine lot of articles, we call walking sticks
I should liked to have prigged one, but a still voice whispered no
The bobbies will cop you at Bellingham Show.

There was leaping for horses o'er hurdle and fence
The pluck of the riders and horses immense
They leapt like the deer when he hears the horn blow
Winning rosy bright laurels at Bellingham show.

The farmers looked happy the wools had a rise
The lambs have sold well, the ewes will likewise
Their bright smiling faces as they walked to and fro
Bespoke of contentment at Bellingham show.

The young lads and lassies in glee swung and danced
And from eye unto eye, the love lightening quick glanced
Many a King of Creation, whether Tom, Dick or Joe
Plighted vows with his Donah at Bellingham show.

Tis a day when young Cupid throws forth many darts
And transfixes them deep in the young peoples hearts
There many a young damsel, that day gets a beau
Who ne'er had a sweetheart before Bellingham show.

Old friends here clasp hands with a hearty good will
And talk of old times o'er a glass or a gill
They've not met for a twelvemonth, and who is to know
They'll perhaps not meet again till next Bellingham Show.

The cur dogs on the showyard did grumble and growl
As the hounds up at Newton sent up a great howl
These brave tried old warriors every one of them know
They meet the next morn after Bellingham show.

May Sol's smile long fall on old Tyne's crystal stream
And nay fair Redesdale still catch the glint of his beam
May sweet laughing plenty to them ever flow
And success crown the efforts of Bellingham show.

The next morning awoke, and with joy unconfined
Contentment on Natures fair bosom reclined
To the meet with the border, many Nimrods did go
Who had courted the pleasures of Bellingham show.

Brave Robson rode forth in the pride of the morn
Just after the smile of sweet Phoebus was born
The cry of his dogs and his loud tally ho
Far eclipsed all the joys of the Bellingham Show.

90   *14 Apr 1904*

JOHN STEELS GATE

Sent to Mr. J. Steel, Otterburn.

'Twas on the first day of April
The wind was blowing half-a-gale
The sleety showers were sweeping past
Driven by the cold and wintry blast
As homeward on my way I went
Sore with hard toil and labour spent
Twas then I saw Steel and his mate
Commence to build an enterance gate.
And taking shelter 'neath the wall
Till past should go the stormy squall

There John and I, we did forgather
To talk about the stormy weather.
There unto John I then did state
We'd name the entrance John Steel's Gate,
Then John to me did answer back
If at poetry I'd been a crack
Its pillars I'd immortalise
Their grace their symmetry and size
The thought then rankled through my pate
To immortalise John Steels new Gate.
The gate stands on the Kings highway
Or rather I had better say
The structure stands upon the wall
Built of the best of freestone all
Its pillars square, a diamond crown
From which the water will run down
A piece of work I must relate
Gives John great credit for this gate.
The gate has not been built for show
But for the use of those who go
Their different pleasures to partake
Upon the Company's new made lake
For those who boat, or those who fish
Or any other sport they wish
It will them all accommodate
They all must pass through John Steels gate.
May well it stand, as years go by
To pierce the future I will try
I see a maid in distant day
Dressed smart in colours bright and gay
She comes along expectantly
And coming round yon bend I see
A young man, who shall say 'twas fate
The trysting place was John Steels gate.

Again I look along the way
I see an old man bent and gray
And leading on with gentle care
A pleasing child, both young and fair

They come within my listening ear
And presently their talk I hear,
Now Johnny Ma will think us late
We'll turn again at John Steels gate.

Now John perhaps when far away
When you have turned both old and gray
When sitting in your ingle's chair
To read your evening paper there
And as its pages o'er you scan
You'll see how yon grief stricken man
His mind unhinged, a desperate fate
Had drowned himself near John Steels gate.
Again you o'er its pages look
This time an accident you brook
When coming from the Carter Bar
Smash went the tourists motor car
Your wife looks up expectantly
And asks the question suddenly
Where did it happen does it state
You answer back near John Steels gate.
Long may it stand to fill its place
And bring its builders no disgrace
Around its base the waves will dash
And o'er its crown the spray shall splash
The wind shall whistle through its space
The showers each other through shall chase
Now Sir I trust to fateful fate
That I've immortalised the gate.

93   *14 Nov 1904*

"THE CLEUGH"

These many years I have been asked
The question every day
As I've been busy at my work
Upon the Kings Highway

42

By navigators o'er the land
In accents kind or bluff
Hey, matey could you tell me now
How far I'm off the "Cleugh".

From North from South from East and West
They've come both near and far
The Sandys from old Scotland
Have crossed the Carter Bar
From lowlands and from highlands
Joch Scott and Neil McDuff
Have all been speiring if I knew
The distance to the "Cleugh".

And from across the ocean
Bould Paddy you may see
With his bundle strapped upon his back
He's tramped from Glasgow Quay
And as he comes along the road
A likely "bhoy" and tough
He stops to say shure mister now
How far is't to the "Cleugh".

Than the John Bulls of England
Of them there's been galore
The Nobbys and the Pinchers
And Punche's many a score
The Lanky's and the Lincolns
Both respectable and rough
Have all enquired how far it was
To this here blooming "Cleugh".

Some of then but stayed a week
Some might stay two or three
And then by that time off they went
For a rodney or a spree
They tell you they can't stick it
Of the job they've had enough
And never more you'll see them back
To work up at the "Cleugh".

In three weeks time you'll see a man
Come slowly on the way
No more he reels along the road
Nor are his spirits gay
Helloo you say you're back again
He answers low and gruff
I wish I'd never left the job
I had up at the "Cleugh".

I've been up at the Tallow
And I've been to Morecambe Bay
I've tried the Clyde I've tried the Forth
And I've been to the Tay
The work was hard the pay was small
And many a sharp rebuff
I only hope I'll get a job
When I get to the "Cleugh".

How that the works are near complete
The Navvies all declare
They never worked upon a job
Where payment was so fair
The "tommy" fit for any Prince
Roast beef and rich plum duff
Soon made them all both sleek and fat
When working at the "Cleugh".

In time to come when navvies meet
Upon some distant job
They'll cast their minds back o'er the years
That time doth from us rob
And as they there each other pledge
In a drop of prime old stuff
They'll talk upon the happy days
They had up at the "Cleugh".

"WHIST" ON THE HUNT AFTER THE "WOLF"

A well known scribbler of the North
From gay Newcastle sallied forth
To hunt "the wolf" in regions far
Well mounted on a motor car
And as he on did swiftly glide
In anxious frame of mind he cried
    I hunt the wolf,

As through each village street he passed
The motor horn sent forth a blast
The people all did look and stare
To see a man with snowy hair
Who waved his sinewy arm on high
And shouted with a kindling eye
    I hunt the wolf.

He listened to the woodmans tale
In many a lone sequestered dale
The keepers each their story told
Which made the huntsman brave and bold
He stood up in his motor car
And cried in thunders sounding far
    I hunt the wolf.

High up upon the hills he went
And oft his anxious eye was bent
In searching all the landscape wide
But ne'er the wild dog he espied
From mountain valley hill and plain
The echoes sounded back again
    I hunt the wolf.

O rest admirers cried and take
A little for thy stomachs sake
The huntsman growing gray and old
Felt wintry winds both chill and cold

And as he raised his glass on high
Again was heard the well known cry
    I hunt the wolf.

O stay the ladies cried and rest
Thy snowy head upon this breast
He placed his hand upon his heart
To stay the thrusts of Cupids dart
He cast on them a longing eye
And from him there escaped the sigh
    But for the wolf.

When at the close of winters day
He turned him homeward on his way
Advice from friends he proud did scorn
To rest until the coming morn
Beware the beast the people cried
A voice far in the night replied
    There is no wolf.

Next morning at the break of day
Stark stiff and cold the huntsman lay
The jury twelve good men and true
Proceed his poor corpse to view
And as his mangled form they 'spied
In lamentations loud they cried
    Killed by the wolf.

(On 17 Dec 1904 the Hexham Courant reported that a wolf had been sighted in Allendale as well as tracks in the snow and dead sheep. After further sightings it reported on 14 January that a wolf had been killed by a train near Cumwhinton, across the moors from Allendale)

FANCY MOTOR CARS

Its a stirring age we're living in
This fact none can deny
And soon a horse and trap will be
Things of the days gone bye
Our roads now must be clean and smooth
And free from jolts and jars
For all the rage in travelling is
By fancy motor cars.

Through dust and heat, through mud and rain
You seen them onward rush
In early morn, in noontides glare
And evenings gentle hush
In spite of "Peelers" and of laws
There's nothing them debars
From rushing to destruction
In their fancy motor cars.

And don't they all look "awfully nice"
With goggles on their eyes
A curious muzzle on their mouths
To keep out dust and flies
Their German sausage caps would suit
The firey sons of Mars
More than the peaceful citizens
In their fancy motor cars,

At one time it was thought correct
And quite up to the mark
To take out dear Angela
For a canter in the park
But nowadays tis different
For all the mighty stars
Take out their tootsy wootsys
In their fancy motor cars.

The ladies now ne'er list the birds
That sing so sweet at morn
The only music that they love's
The braying motor horn
No thoughts have they of serenades
Or lovers with guitars
But only blokes who'll take them out
In their fancy motor cars.

An soon I fear the Mary Janes
Who once had hearts quite warm
Will pout upon a fellow
Should he offer them his arm
For when they have their "evening out"
They'll scorn the poor Jack Tars
And go off with the chauffeurs
In their fancy motor cars.

The lord, the squire, the statesman
Have all now caught the flame
The editor and many more
Too numerous to name
And when again we shall go forth
To fight our bloody wars
We'll send out Tommy Atkins
In our fancy motor cars.

101   *14 July 1905*

THE BRIDAL TEA POT

Come all ye who by Cupids dart
Have been transfixed deep through heart
Advice take from a fellow mortal
If you would enter Hymens portal
Now start at once for Birdhopecraig
By motor car or spanking naig

Where lives a priest who'll tie the knot
And give the bride a new Teapot.

And when your honeymoon you've spent
And billed and cooed your hearts content
When you your little home have stocked
In double harness fairly yoked
Now every Sunday please remember
As the kettle sings above your ember
Take from its weekly resting spot
And hansel then your new Teapot.

It may be soon it may be later
You'll be a mater or a pater
And when old friends drop in to see
Who like the little one may be
And when they praise its matchless beauty
Why then you'll find it is your duty
A cup of tea both strong and hot
To serve out of your new Teapot.

And should his reverence some fine day
A welcome visit to you pay
Cut off a rasher from your ham
Bring out your marmalade and jam
Some barley cakes and white loaf bread
And with your table thus well spread
You wont forget I surely wot
To mask the tea in your bridal pot.

Now when you've turned both old and grey
And many friends have passed away
When nearing to that certain bourne
From which no traveller can return
Give then into the trustful care
Of her your first sweet babe so fair
And counsel her what e'er her lot
To cherish well your bridal pot.

And to each coming generation
May it be a thing of veneration
And if among far distant climes
Their lot be cast in future times
Perchance amid the frigid snows
Or where the sun sheds torrid glows
Long after we are all forgot
They'll reverence there your bridal pot

115   *No date*

A RUN WITH A. SALMON

The rain had ceased and from the East
The wind had westward shifted
And moving high across the sky
The grey clouds lazily drifted
With rod and reel and willow creel
I hied me to the river
Whose waters brown kept pouring down
In ceaseless currents ever.

My cast I fixed with feelings mixed
Of doubt and expectation
Uncertain I which noted fly
Best suited the occasion
But luck was mine for scarce the line
Had landed on the water
When there arose a salmon's nose
And seized the hook with hauteur.

The reel sang out without a doubt
He was a twenty pounder
He tugged and splashed then onward dashed
With many a leap and flounder
I gave him line, no thought was mine
To strain my rod and tackle

For well I knew, that soon adieu
'Twould be to cast and hackle.

Now o'er the stream I saw him gleam
His glorious colours shining
I did my best but still suppressed
The thought to pull inclining
Then for yon bush he made a rush
And tried his best to enter
I was perforce, for good or worse
More pressure now to venture.

His struggles ceased my strain increased
As o'er the stream he floated
Upon his side and gasping wide
I o'er my prize now gloated
Next in the pool he tried to rule
And then became quite sulky
And down below I felt him go
His weight and size both bulky.

Then like a log stuck in a bog
He lay there without motion
A sulkier fish ne'er graced a dish
Or swam the briny ocean
I held him tight and gave him weight
Till of these tactics tiring
He upward jumped then downward plumped
To liberty aspiring.

His strength now failed and I prevailed
And wound the line up steady
As to the shore I pulled him o'er
With fatal gaff hook ready
A yard, a foot, and then ah! but
His waning strength reviving
Away he went on purpose bent
Amid the stream arriving.

Again I wound and soon I found
Once more I was his master
My hopes rose high that surely I
Was now free from disaster
So inch by inch came line to winch
He now was fairly stranded
I had my wish, I gaffed my fish
And safely I him landed.

119   *14 March 1905*

TO THE DIPPER

Frequenter of the rippling rills
Thou restless monarch of the brooks
Away amid the peaceful hills
Thy life is spent in quiet nooks.

Thy throat and breast of snowy white
Thy back of deep dark dingy brown
Thy beady eyes of lustre bright
Like diamonds shine in regal crown.

From place to place thou constant flits
Nor for a moment can keep still
And when upon a stone thou sits
Thou makes thy bows unto the rill.

And with the music making streams
Thou raisest sweet thy tuneful part
Commingling with their happy themes
The great desires of thy heart,

More genial climes thou seekest not
But braves the winters angry frown
Where Nature gave to thee thy lot
Thou reignest o'er the waters brown.

In early Spring thou builds thy nest
And cunningly thou weaves the moss
Upon some favoured rock 'tis pressed
Where underneath the waters toss.

Thy tender brood are early hatched
Ere other birds their eggs have layed
Thee oft them feeding I have watched
When first primroses deck the glade.

And when I looked within thy nest
I saw four yellow opened beaks
Sure little bird thou'll get no rest
They'll find thee work for coming weeks.

Thy consorts of the Summer day
The piper, martin and wagtail
In Winter do not with thee stay
Less rigorous climates then they hail.

Reign on thou monarch of the rills
Contentment seems to be thy lot
And if this virtue thy heart fills
Alas! by man 'tis oft forgot.

136   *June 1905*

THE FISHING ADVENTURE OF JIMMY HASTIE

In a neat little village the name I won't tell
Jimmy Hastie and Betty, his good wife did dwell
As loving a couple as well you might see
But on one knotty subject, they could not agree.
For Jimmy was passionately fond of trout fishing
And Betty was ever and constantly wishing
That her spouse would stay more at home and keep warm
Lest by getting wet feet, his health should take harm.

It happened one time Betty kept him in bed
With a very bad cough, and a cold in his head
When Maggie, their daughter took suddenly ill
Though not with an ailment that was likely to kill
But one that was calculated to bring them joy rather
For it ended by Jimmy becoming grandfather.
So Betty went off to look after her daughter
And charged Jimmy well not to go to the water
Of course he then promised he'd lie snug in bed
And pay great attention to what Betty said.

That summer the weather had been very dry
Scarce a cloud had appeared in the bright azure sky
But the day before the rain had poured down
And made all the rivers and brooks a dark brown
So Jimmy resolved once his Betty away
He'd have a day's fishing the very next day.
Of course he'd be careful and not wet his feet
And go to some peaceful and quiet retreat
Away 'mid the hills where the streams were preserved
And where by the Keepers he'd not be observed.

So early next morning at break of the day
He stole like a thief from his cottage away
The bright sun arose o'er the top of the hills
And gladsomely shone on the sweet flowing rills
With a heart that was light and a mind free from care
Jimmy stept briskly forth in the fresh morning air.
Two hours of good walking brought Jimmy at last
Where he thought he might safely fix up rod and cast
And soon the enjoyment which anglers feel
Was his as the beauties were placed in his creel.

The winged time flew past as sweet hours surely will
Still further and further he went up the rill
And Jimmy felt glorious for care he had none
Till he uncautiously stept on a treacherous stone
He tried all he knew his equilibrium to save
Then suddenly dashed in the swift flowing wave

Well up to his middle he stood in the pool
And O but the water felt chilly and cool
Then like a poor cat that is nearly half drowned
He scrambled his way till he reached the dry ground.

Ah! well thought poor Jimmy the weather is warm
I'll put off my trousers I'll not take the least harm
And if round my shoulders I had them loose tied
In a very short time the things will get dried.
So off went his trousers and there he stept forth
Like the men of the mountains bred far in the North
Though what was his tartan and what was his clan
Would have puzzled the brains of the best highlandman
No sporran he wore and no gay coloured plaid
And his strong sturdy calves were by hose unarrayed
But like a true man Fortune's frown he did meet
And thankful he felt in this quiet retreat
There was no one his pitiful plight to behold
And no Betty at home to him ruthlessly scold.

But soon he forgot all his woes for a while
As the trouts began taking his bait in fine style
But feeling quite hungry and tired at last
He wound up his line and fastened his cast
Then climbed the hill side to a spring he well knew
To eat there his luncheon and take in the view.
But what Jimmy saw did him greatly surprise
And scarcely could he believe his own eyes
Yet there was no doubt for there he espied
The much dreaded Keeper come o'er the hillside.

Like a hare Jimmy bounded when beagles pursue
And o'er the rough heath as for dear life he flew
As a high blooded hunter the Keeper gave chase
But soon far behind he was left in the race
On on went our hero and ne'er looked behind
For to outwit the Keeper he'd made up his mind
He dodged in behind all the trees and the rocks
Sagacious and cunning as an oft hunted fox

Till at last in his ears he could hear the loud din
Where the waters rushed wild o'er a steep rocky lynn
So hastily hiding rod, trousers and creel
He fixed on a place his own self to conceal.
Without more ado to a pool he sprang in
Where the cold water reached just up to us chin
Well up 'neath some rocks where a welcome bush grew
Which kept well his face and his wet hair from view.

The Keeper came up and he searched all around
But nothing of Jimmy was there to be found
Until he espied behind a green sod
His much draggled trousers, his creel and his rod.
Ah well thought the Keeper the rascals away
I'll just gather together my own lawful prey
He admiringly took up the rod and the reel
And gingerly Jimmy's wet trousers did feel
A smile crossed his face for his critical view
Revealed him the fact that though wet they were new
So over his shoulders he slung them with pride
And went on his way o'er the heathy hill side.

Now Jimmy began old dame Fortune to scold
Though the weather was warm yet the water was cold
So he ventured to look if the Keeper was gone
And quickly discovered that he was there alone.
Now out from concealment he slyly did steal
To look for his trousers his rod and his creel
And O what great horror was fixed in his mind
As he naught of his tackle and garments could find
So slowly and sadly he onward did stray
And oft longed for darkness to banish the day
For he hoped to reach home under cover of night
Where he could not well venture in the glare of daylight

But unexpectedly Fortune again sweetly smiled
Whose treatment he'd deep and wrathfully reviled
Jimmy looked on with wonder as a sight met his eyes
Which filled him with pleasure as well as surprise

For there was a garden, and there too our friend
The gentleman scarecrow to his duties did tend

He was drest up in garments that fitted his sphere
Not of the last fashion by many a year
He wore a long coat near a century old
The buttons now brass might at one time be gold
Its colour had boasted a bright Lincoln green
But now it was dingy and ragged I ween
He wore a long topper with a very broad brim
Which at one time no doubt looked both natty and trim
His trousers which Jimmy looked lovingly on
Were a godsend to a man who such garments had none
Their length was but scanty and as Jimmy could see
They wouldn't reach more than an inch past his knee
But then he was needful and this could descry
Though ill fitting his person, yet they surely were dry.

With his hand on the pale Jimmy sprung at the fence
But unable to bear his proportions immense
Without any warning rail gave a crack
And Jimmy fell prone on the broad of his back
High up in the air flew his long naked shins
Then caressed in descending a strong bush of whins
Which prickled immensely and his tender skin tore
And though a good Christian I fear Jimmy swore
Still smarting and wrathful again he arose
And proceeded to take from the scarecrow his clothes.

The trousers he took off with caution and care
Lest the legs from the seat he should happen to tear
Then with many a struggle he got his limbs dressed
And looked a sorrowful figure it must be confessed
Then fancy suggested, to complete his disguise,
To put on the coat and the topper likewise
No knight of the road with his blanket and bags
Was e'er clothed in a dress of such ragged old rags
And no Weary Willie what e'er his degree
Better clad for the calling of a gaberlundsie

In the shade of the evening as homeward he passed
Many pityful glances upon him were cast
In safety he went down his own village street
Many well known faces he happened to meet
But none recognised as he plainly could see
Their well known good neighbour Mr. Jimmy Hastie.

Now Jimmy imagined his troubles were o'er
As he joyfully went to his own cottage door
But alas! that such fancies had ever been born
They perished at once 'neath his own Betty's scorn
Begone you old beggar she wrathfully cried
As to make his way past her the wretched man tried
Thieves, murder and robbers she excitedly screamed
That 'twas her own husband old Betty ne'er dreamed
She'd hurried across from her daughters that night
Just to see that her Jimmy was keeping all right
She found the house closed so sat down at the door
To nurse her impatience, what could she do more
But when Jimmy spoke her fears were assuaged
She well know that voice, but O how she raged
She called him for all the old idiots and fools
He'd broken his promise, and defied all her rules
Jimmy opened the door with all haste that he could
For in a short time he well knew that there would
Be a crowd of their neighbours to hear their dispute
And he'd much for to answer, that he could not refute
So into the cottage Betty followed her Hector
Determined to give him a much needed lecture.

In silence sat Jimmy, not a word did he speak
His poor flesh was willing but his spirit was weak
And he very well knew from experience of old
The more his excuses, the more she would scold
And Jimmy well reasoned, and a wise man was he
If it pleases old Betty, it doesn't harm me
In haste he proceeded to put off his old rags
While as a clock pendulum old Betty's tongue wags

58

But when she saw his wet garments beneath
Her rage was unbounded and she gnashed with her teeth
Into bed she got Jimmy and in dry clothing dressed
And he then with much prudence his adventures confessed
And Betty but human began now to laugh
At the story unfolded by her own better half.

Then Jimmy began to enquire for his daughter
While to his feet Betty placed, a warm bottle of water
The news which she told him, filled his old heart with joy
When he heard that his Maggie had got a fine boy
And over his face did the sweetest smile gather
When told that the babe should be named for Grandfather.

But being quite weary Jimmy fell asleep sound
And snored with an energy great and profound
Yet his dreams seemed unpleasant for now and again
He struggled and moaned as if suffering pain
No doubt in his mind the poor tired old sleeper
Still thought he was chased by cunning old Keeper.

However next morning he woke in good time
And to Betty's enquiry said he was feeling quite prime
As at breakfast they sat Jimmy promised his wife
As regarding the fishing they'd have no more strife.
So back to their daughters again Betty went
Leaving Jimmy at home of his sins to repent.

They now live quite happy his wife's had her wish
Never more has her Jimmy gone out for to fish
But oft when he strays down the neat village street
And happens his friend the old Keeper to meet
While listening to one of that worthies long speeches
He casts longing eyes on his own well known breeches.

TO THE FIRST SWALLOW 1905

Thou art come again o'er the oceans wave
With thy glossy pinions spread
To sport where the crystal streamlets lave
To the summers fairy tread.

Thou hast spent our cold and winters day
In some sunny genial clime
Where the groves are decked with the orange spray
And the wealth of the juicy vine.

Where the green trees live in endless bloom
And the flowerets never die
Where no cloud or darkness casts its gloom
O'er the face of the azure sky.

Where the sparkling fountains rainbows make
'Neath the suns celestial smile
By the golden sands of the glittering lake
The home of the crocodile.

Perchance on the banks of the Nile methinks
Thou hast skimmed the palms amid
Or looked on the face of the wondrous sphinx
And soared o'er the Pyramid.

With the lightenings speed o'er the briny deep
Thou hast come at the summers call
To build thy nest on some frowning Keep
Or some rural cottage wall.

And we welcome thee back to this land of ours
To chatter 'neath our eaves
To share with us the time of flowers
And our forests filled with leaves.

AMID THE HILLS OF REDESDALE.

Now Phoebus with his kindly beams
Smiles sweet on woodlands, fields and streams
Where happy songsters chant their themes
Amid the hills of Redesdale.

Now with radiant stately mein
Summer spreads her mantle green
Where the new shorn flocks are seen
Amid the hills of Redesdale.

Where the many coloured flowers
Sparkling with the dewy showers
Lighten up the fragrant bowers
Amid the hills of Redesdale.

Leafy woods and ferny fells
Time worn deep and rocky dells
Clear cold bubbling crystal wells
Amid the hills of Redesdale.

Where the heath bedecks the wold
Where the sunsets sink in gold
O'er the mountains grim and old
Amid the hills of Redesdale.

Majestic rude and towering rocks
Hanging o'er in shapeless blocks
Where doth lurk the cunning fox
Amid the hills of Redesdale.

Where the huntsman's horn doth blow
Where is heard the view haloo
And the rousing tally hoo
Amid the hills of Redesdale.

Where the pricker once did ride
Trusty broad sword by his side
Moon and stars his only guide
Amid the hills of Redesdale.

Where the hut and sheltering Peel
Oft the touch of fire did feel
When the Scotsmen came to steal
Amid the hills of Redesdale.

Where the din of battle brayed
Where drank deep the flashing blade
Deeds of valour were displayed
Amid the hills of Redesdale.

But these times have changed today
Blessed peace now holds her sway
May she reign for ay and ay
Amid the hills of Redesdale.

(Pricker is an old name for a horseman with spurs and hence a reiver)

148   *1 Aug 1905*

MODERN JUGGERNAUT CARS

They come they come in a cloud of dust
You can hear their war steeds neigh
As filled with a mad and unlawful lust
They search o'er the Kings Highway
And leave behind a trail of blood
Of the innocents they have slain
O! how shall we stem that deep red flood
And our safety once more regain
Ho! these are the demons let loose on earth
By the firey god of wars
To kill and slay on the Kings Highway
By their modern Juggernaut Cars.

They come they come through the rural vale
And they charge through the village street
With the speed and noise of the merciless gale
They seek out each blest retreat
Their firey eyes neath the midnight skies
Like the fearsome dragon's shine
And the breath from their nostrils upward flies
Like the stench of a gassy mine
Ho! these are the demons let loose on earth
By the firey god of wars
To kill and slay on the Kings Highway
By their modern Juggernaut Cars.

They come they come from the North and South
They come from the East and the West
And the white foam flies from their steaming mouth
And flakes on their panting chest
Their thunders shake the quaking road
As they pant up the steepest hill
Spurred on by their fierce and begoggled load
Who urge them at their will
Ho! these are the demons let loose on earth
By the firey god of wars
To kill and slay on the Kings Highway
By their modern Juggernaut Cars.

153   *219   No date*

THE NIGHT WE SPENT IN COQUET WATTER

The skies were grey that winters day
And doon the rain did ceaseless splatter
My friend and me we did agree
To spend a night in Coquet watter.

Ower hills and howes tae Lounges Knows
Abraid the auld yowes we did scatter
And made a pledge on Riddlees edge
We'd hae some fun in Coquet watter.

Down Riddlees burn, we took the turn
Twas roond aboot, what did it matter
Wie oor frien' Tam we had a dram
O' something mixed wie Coquet watter.

Then on we went on purpose bent
And soon the miles we ower did batter
Till unco croose, the auld school hoose
We spied close tae the Coquet watter.

When we gat there snug in the chair
Our worthy Nimrod, growing fatter
Presided o'er, as oft of yore
That gala night in Coquet watter.

Our auld frien' Jim was in fine trim
O' lang nebbed words he has a smatter
To parliment he should be sent
To represent auld Coquet wetter.

Wie merry sang the rafters rang
The speeches were na ment tae flatter
That night on earth, dear social mirth
Smiled sweetest on auld Coquet watter.

The concert oer, upon the floor
Stood stalward son and bonnie daughter
With eyes sae bright and hearts sae light
The flower and pride O' Coquet watter.

The fiddle squeeled, around we wheeled
The lassies feet went pitter patter
Nae waists sae sma' nane drest sae braw
As the fair young queens O' Coquet watter.

The shepherd men frae hill and glen
Their brass nebbed shoon did clitter clatter
And flang their heels in jigs and reels
That night we spent in Coquet watter.

Ae, fine young queen, wie bonnie e'en
I spiered her age an' what they ca't her
Says she my man, ne'er try your han'
We're ower fly in Coquet watter.

Dame Fortune smiled and ne'er beguiled
That fickle jade we mauna' fau't her
The sweet hours flew, before we knew
The morning dawned o'er Coquet watter.

We had a feed o' fancy bread
But Oh! we wished for something sauter
Our mouths were wairsh oor throats were hairsh
Wie the night we spent in Coquet watter.

Then through the fields to Battleshields
Wie our frien' Wat we had a chatter
And with a glass we pledged each lass
And a' the folks in Coquet watter.

Then o'er the hill wie right good will
We gaily sang "Wha' is your hatter"
Baith weel content, a night we'd spent
Wie canty folks o' Coquet watter.

AN OLD SHEPHERD'S ADVENTURE AT BELLINGHAM SHOW
1905

Aw am an a'd herd and aw live far oot bye
Aw seldom see owt but the sheep and the kye
So Aw says tiv wor Betsy Aw think Aw will go
To hev a bit leuk at the Bellingham Show.

Ah weel, says the a'd wife, if the money's to spare
No doot it's a lang time since ye hev been there.
Wor pack lambs hev seld weel, they've a lang time been low
So Aw think ye might gan tiv the Bellingham Show.

So Aw gets mesel' drest in me braw Sunday claes
And me brass nebbed shoon polished black as twa shaes,
A big stand up collar, and me tie in a bo'
Aw looked quite a masher at Bellingham Show.

Well Aw got tiv the show ground, and managed first rate
And paid me bit shilling to git in at the gate.
Aw met wie some a'd friends who cried oot hal-lo
Hes thou really gitten, tiv Bellingham Show.

Aw was feeling gay dry so in we all went
Just tae hev a wee drop an a crack in the tent,
Aw said mine was a half but the rest all cried no
There's to be no half glasses at Bellingham Show.

Well we all had a glass or it might hev been two
Or to tell ye the real truth, we maybe hed three,
The wee drop that we got set oor heart in a glow
As we talked ower a'd times at Bellingham Show.

Aw then hed a look at the tups and the hoggs
The horses, the cows, the fat pigs and the dogs,
And all ower the showfield Aw went to and fro
Determined to miss nowt at Bellingham Show.

Aw got me eye on a chap that was selling half croons
There wad nee body buy them but Aw thout they were cloons
The fook all did laugh as they stood in a row
When Aw bought three for two shillings at Bellingham Show.

When Aw opened the purse to take oot the tin
Aw saw at a glance Aw was weel taken in
A brass broach and two pennies, how ma temper did grow
When Aw saw aw'd been cheated at Bellingham Show,

Aw was hevin' a look at the butter and eggs
And sat doon on some boxes to ease me a'd legs,
Up comes a fine lady fat, forty and slow
Contented and jolly at Bellingham Show.

Excuse me she says but I do hate mistakes
Now which are the duck eggs and which are the drake's,
I just have been wondering, I thought ye might know
There's intelligent people at Bellingham Show.

Aw can tell ye that Mistress, it's quite plain to be seen
The duck eggs are white and the drake ones is green,
Oh! how simple, she cried, and how wise one may grow
By making enquiries at Bellingham Show.

Aa stept up to a chap what was shaved tiv the lips
Says Aw, canny man, three pennorth o' chips.
He cursed and he sent me to the regions below
He was a motor car driver at Bellingham Show.

Excuse me, cries Aw, but Aw doot Aw am green
Aa thought ye were minding a fried chip machine,
Whey man that's a motor belongs Lord So and So
And we're hevin a day at the Bellingham Show.

So Aw dodged away round by the edge o' the crood
And smoked me a'd pipe in a nice happy mood,
When up comes a young queen and cries oot Uncle Joe
I am glad to have met you at Bellingham Show.

She flung her arms roond me neck and gav me a kiss
And Oh! tiv an a'd man nee doot it was bliss
But Aw wasn't her uncle and aw told her straight so
That Aw hadn't a niece at the Bellingham Show.

She gave a bit scream and Aw thout she wad faint
But Aw sometimes jaloose that the women folks paint.
Oh excuse me says she, and your pardon bestow
Mistakes sometimes happen at Bellingham Show.

It's all right now hinny it's all right Aw did cry
While Aw stooped down a minute me shoelaces to tie.
When Aw looked up again and me eyes roond did throw
Me relation had vanished at Bellingham Show.

Me heart begen jumpin and Aw felt fairly spent
So Aw thowt Aw wad hev a bit glass in the tent,
So inside Aw got, felt ma pockets and lo
That fly jade had robbed me at Bellingham Show.

Not a copper Ad left not a cent did remain
And gean were ma a'd specks ma watch and ma chain
The watch Aw had bowt masel lang years ago
When Aw first courted Betsy at Bellingham Show

Well Aw went tiv the Bobby an telt him me tale
But he said Aw was nowt but a silly a'd feul,
Twas time Aw knew better as a'd men should know
Not to meddle the lasses at Bellingham Show.

Aw got see excited and lood Aw did yell
That the policeman took me right off tiv the cell,
Through the door he did send me with the tip o' his toe
Saying "Keep theesel' quiet ower Bellingham Show".

Aw got oot the next morning and made me way hame
But tiv wor a'd wife not a thing did Aw name
She'll knaw suen enough they'll be plenty to blow
Aboot me misfortunes at Bellingham Show,

Now Aw've a blue paper and it says that next week
Aw hev to appear 'fore his worship the beak
Seven days teasing oakum Oh! My poor heart is low
Aw'll gan ne mair back tiv the Bellingham Show.

165   *2 Nov 1905*

BETTY McPHEE

There lives an old maiden named Betty McPhee
Who once was the sweetest young lass you could see
She dwelt with her father who kept a small farm
And he loved his dear lassie with a heart that was warm
And her dear doting mother with her pa did agree
That a match for a lord was Miss Betty McPhee.

Near where Betty lived a young squire did dwell
And there was the parson and doctor as well
So she made up her mind well coached by her mother
If she could not get one she would try for the other
No misgivings had she, but that one of these three
Should be the dear husband of Betty McPhee.

She oft met the squire abroad in his grounds
Who went forth a sporting with gun or with hounds
With Betty he flirted nor thought it amiss
To imprint on her red lips that thing called a kiss
His love she ne'er doubted, but a sad dog was he
And played the deceiver with Betty McPhee.

So trustful was Betty, that she never did tire
In sounding the praise of her lover the squire
And pictured herself, by the end of the fall
The fine stately lady, who reigned at the Hall
But he married a yankee from over the sea
And left broken hearted Miss Betty McPhee.

But one ray of comfort Betty had yet, at least
She would now try her hand on his reverence the priest
And it must be confessed that he was not averse
The part of a lover with her to rehearse
And often they met, was it accidently
His reverence the parson and Betty McPhee.

Betty's hopes now rose high she'd be settled for life
In a neat little home as a clergyman's wife
But with the sly priest, she was ne'er to be matched
Betty counted her chickens before they were hatched
For he choose an old widow quite on the Q.T.
Who had matter, O, moneyial charms more than Betty McPhee

Next to the young doctor Betty turned a sharp eye
And often felt vexed that he should be so shy
But alas! something happened that made Betty weep
He took some strong chloral to send him to sleep
He ne'er woke again so it's as plain as can be
He'll ne'er be the husband of Betty McPhee.

Betty had many suitors nice decent young men
But she scorned them all as beneath her great ken
She looked out for gallants, but past they have ridden
She gazed at the moon till she fell in the midden
She now is a wanter at fifty and three
And still remains hopeful Miss Betty McPhee.

She is willing to marry if only she can
Get anything just half the shape of a man
She isn't particular to the shade of his skin
A tall man a small man fat, medium or thin
A black man a red man a heathen Chinee
Would gladly be welcomed by Betty McPhee.

MY BONNIE SHEPHERD LAD

Oh! I love yon rocky mountains, and I love yon winding glen
For there doth roam my Willie to me the king of men
With his twa good faithful doggies, and roond his neck his plaid
Tae me there's nane that's dearer, than my bonnie shepherd lad

Qh! I met him in the summer down in yon birky bower
When the mavis sang his love song in the twilight's blissful hour
'Twas not the thrilling mavis, that made my heart feel glad
But the story that was told me, by my bonnie shepherd lad.

He told me that he loved me and I took it not amiss
For O to live wie Willie indeed it would be bliss
In some wee bit moorland cottage, I never should feel sad
But aye be blythe and cheery wie my bonnie shepherd lad.

Should Fortune smile upon us. and bless us baith wie health
If she dinna send us riches, yet what care I for wealth
There's mony a wife been happy, who riches never had
Blest wie a loving husband like my bonnie shepherd lad.

And if Heaven should but send us a bonnie lad and lass
But that may be a joy that will never come to pass
But should it then my laddie shall named be for his dad
There's nane can be more worthy, than my bonnie shepherd lad.

LETTER TO:- MR. WILKIE DODD,
Beaufort Rise. Monmouthshire.　　　7th December, 1905

My Dear old Friend,
　　I pray you attend
I will answer your letter in rhyme

For to write you in prose, Sir great goodness knows
It would take up too much of my time.

I am glad Sir to hear, as you quite make it clear
Again you are busy navvy driving
'Mong the Nobbies and Bens, and th' ring tailed Siens
And other funny names most surprising.

No doubt the old hands, one quite understands
Will not like to be "bossed" by a stranger
Don't show the white feather, and the storm you will weather
And soon steer your ship clear of danger.

You're now far from the hills, and bonnie bonnie rills
And far from the friends you hold dear
Who often think on you, and wish you success
With hearts that are leal and sincere.

And we trust Sir that you, to us will be true
That often fond fancy will stray
Back to the valley so peaceful and still
And the friends now so far far way.

May prosperity smile on the work of your hands
And Fortune come quick at your call
If she don't bring you wealth Oh! may she bring health
The best greatest blessing of all.

But should the Dame frown, and her visage look brown
You must face her dear friend like a man
Ne'er meet trouble half way, howe'er black the day
But strive for the top if you can.

And if you should find, a queen to your mind
Amid the wild mountains of Wales
May she bring you delight, she is yours Sir by right
For the women were made for the males.

And if on your knee, you should dandle in glee
Twin babies - a sister and brother
Call the boy for yourself, and the other young elf
Why call it old chap for its mother.

On Tuesday last, mid the stormy blast
Your bike passed along on a cart
To see it go by, Oh! I nearly did cry
For the sight Sir quite melted my heart.

I thought on the times I had seen it go past
With good old Dodd it astride
And the many happy days, and different ways
We often and merrily did ride.

As to news in the vale there's a not much to detail
But this much I truly can say
At Elisha Farm a fire careered in its ire
And consumed Jimmy Davidsons hay.

But he had it insured, so it can be endured
As well and verily it should
For instead of a loss, I believe he'll be close
Unto twenty pounds to the good.

Our friend Thomas Brydon, we'll now see astride on
A hunter and following the hounds
'Lisha Farm he has taken and soon will awaken
The vale with his musical sounds.

The Angel of death hath been in our midst
John Hedley is with us no more
He sleepeth at rest, and perhaps it is best
Although we his sad loss deplore.

Whilst some have been sad there's others been glad
For such are the workings of Fate
Our neighbour Bill Dagg didn't let his love lag
But is married to his darling Kate.

I have oft been to see, your late landlady
And Meggie with her eyes bright and blue
She's expecting you soon, and perhaps the next moon
May bring you again to her view.

Don't neglect now and than, a line from your pen
To convey how your health Sir is keeping
And may the Great Powers, watch over your hours
Whether resting or working or sleeping.

Now Sir, I must close, and seek some repose
In health I may say I am well
Till I see you again I will constant remain
                    Yours faithfully.
                            WILLIAM BELL.

173   *13 Dec 1905*

A WEE BIT COTTAGE O' MY AIN

Down in yon grove a maiden sang
And this was aye her sweet refrain
Oh! had I but a husband dear
And a wee bit cottage o' my ain.

I'd darn his stockings wash his claes
And never feel life's care or pain
For love would lighten a' my work
In a wee bit cottage o' my ain.

I'd keep my hoosie neat and clean
A wed swept floor a white hearth stane
A smiling face for my guid man
In a wee bit cottage o' my ain.

Nae queen in a' her regal state
Surrounded by her courtly train
Could be mair happy than wad I
In a wee bit cottage o' my ain.

Yet why should I such castles build
For they may tumble down again
As ne'er a lad has asked me yet
To grace a cottage o' my ain.

Yet what is life if without love
A dreary waste a trackless plain
But Oh what bliss 'twould be to have
A wee bit cottage o' my ain.

174   *14 Dec 1905*

A BACCHANAL'S LAMENT

The sky doth frown, the rain comes down
In torrents ceaseless falling
I'm on the roam and far from home
My case is most appalling
Across the Bar, the prospects are
I'll get a proper drenching
With spirits low, I'm filled with woe
From strong potations quenching.

A mason I, I'm always dry
The dust gets in my throttle
If I anoint in every joint
With whiskey from the bottle
The more I drink I sometimes think
My throat but gets the dryer
The more I get you safe may bet
The more do I desire.

Oh! dear Oh! dear my head feels queer
My arms and limbs are shaking
I sadly moan and every bone
Within my frame is aching
And after me in hellish glee
Are fearsome spirits flocking
Above below, their eyebalds glow
My sad condition mocking.

I often think I'll stop the drink
But it has proved my master
If I don't mend, 'twill surely end
In bringing me disaster
I know this well, and oft rebel
But when again I'm tempted
I loose my strength and soon at length
I feel my pockets emptied.

176   *12 Dec 1905*

STOVEY TATTOES

A man o' might is Niddy Wight
His tale I'll tell you gratis
And what tae you I'll swear is true
O' him and stovey tattoes.

Nid is a man ye'll understan'
Wha pawkey as a cat is
He cocks his noose and nowt will choose
But famous stovey tattoes.

Some in their greed on roast beef feed
And some on stewed tomatoes
But gie tae Nid full tae the lid
A pan o' storey tattoes.

On ham and tea he's taen the gee
He says that bacon saut is

And sausage fried he doon hes cried
For sake o' stovey tattoes.

A bunch o' banes and full o' greans
He was but now he fat is
For every day let come what may
He feeds on stovey tattoes.

Nids waist was sma' Just nowt ava'
Nae mair it now sae flat is
But sticks weel oot, without a doot
It's a' wie stovey tattoes.

And e'en his hair is strang and fair
And sleek now as a rat is
For growing hair Nid dis declare
Theres nowt like stovey tattoes.

Mang a' his mates there's nane him bates
And a' their daily crack is
How Nid can work like any Turk
If fed on stovey tattoes.

He has a wife tae bless his life
A queen wha ne'er at faut is
When hame Nid goes sae weel she knows
He's fond o' stovey tattoes.

Nid is a dad his little lad
A knowing little brat is
And like tae Nid the little kid
Cries oot for stovey tattoes.

I'll say no more my tale is o'er
Lest Niddy should flee at us
There'd be a row to you I'll vow
A' ower his stovey tattoes.

*(Stovey Tattoes is a dish made with potatoes and onions fried in a pan; meat,
usually leftovers, is added with water and simmered. Other vegetables optional.)*

TO MR. W. AMOS, WHITE LEE, ON PRESENTING HIM WITH A WALKING STICK OF HUGE DIMENSIONS

Accept this nibby dear old friend
I hope you'll rightly use it
God help the coo the dog or soo
On which you sair aboose it.

Lang may it bear you o'er the muirs
In sunshine gay or drifting snow
With eident care it should you last
Until you Sir an auld man grow.

And if advancing years should fill
Your body full o' girns and graens
And sair rheumatics burn like fire
Within the marrow o' your banes.

Then lean upon this sturdy staff
To rest your limbs and get your breath
And try tae cheat oot o' his ain
That hungry churl we ca' grim death.

But when he Sir shall nick your craik
As soon or late he surely will
This stick will then a tombstone make
And save a greedy sculptors bill.

And if you carve your name thereon
Whether angels bliss or deils defame us
Generations yet unborn will know
Where sleeps a chiel ca'd Wullie Amos.

SAUNTA CLAUS

On Christmas morn as I did stray
Along the frozen Kings Highway
A little maid with laughing eyes
Blue as the radiant summer skies
Came joyfully along the road
Clasped in her arms a treasured load
Who at my side in glee did pause
Saying dis I dot from Saunta Claus.

Before my gaze this maiden droll
Displayed a rosy faced wee doll
With flaxen hair and garments bright
On which she looked with pure delight
My! what a beauty 'tis I cried
To which the little maid replied
My brudder dot a horse dat draws
A 'ittle cart from Saunta Claus.

We hung our stockings up last night
And never waked till was daylight
Dis morning they were all choke full
And what a job we had to pull
Dis dolly out 'cause she's so tall
And den my stockings are so small
But what d'ye think in pa's and Ma's
Der was naught left by Saunta Claus.

Did 'oo hang your stockings on the line
De same way as I hung up mine
Did Saunta Claus bring aught for you
Cried this maid with the eyes so blue
No my sweet dear I did repeat
Den I will give 'oo this nice sweet
I 'oves 'oo well and all because
'Oos wiskers got like Saunta Claus.

THE GENERAL ELECTION OF 1906

There's been a great commotion
And by its powerful blast
Our enemies the Tories
Have been laid low at last
Their flimsy airy fabric
Is a ruined pile of bricks
Through the general election
Of nineteen, nothing, six.

Now their defeated forces
Are filled with grief and woe
Their mighty champion Arthur
Lies buried deep below
With shoddy lime from Birmingham
His mortar he did mix
Which caused this great disaster
In nineteen nothing six.

And where O! where is Joseph?
He lies amid the wreck
A ton of debris on his chest
A corbal on his neck
But still his tongue is wagging
While his heels he upward kicks
And vows he'll yet have vengeance
On nineteen nothing six.

Our leader Campbell Bannerman
This day is feeling proud
As he weaves a flow'ry garland
For Jimmy Arthur's shroud
And looking o'er his shoulder
As his card he doth affix
We read with deepest sympathy
For nineteen nothing six.

Behold the sons of Labour
Triumphantly they come
With flags and banners flying
To the rolling of the drum
They're winning rosy laurels
They're trumping many tricks
In the general election
Of nineteen nothing six.

When they go up to Westminster
We'll find they're men with brains
And very soon we'll feel the hold
They've got upon the reins
They stand upon their merits
No sons of dandy dicks
Who'll represent their comrades
In nineteen nothing six.

The fight will soon be over
And many have been slain
Then let us all with one accord
Unite in peace again
Sink all our party squabbles
Which cling to politics
And work for dear old Britain
In nineteen nothing six.

187   *25 Jan 1906*

A LITTLE GIRL'S TRIP TO LONDON

A little girl of seven who had ne'er left home before
Was taken up to London its wonders to explore
In cab and train she had a ride, on omnibuses too
And lastly on an elephant paraded round the zoo

I expected raptures of delight at the glories of the city
But on my disappointed mind you surely will take pity
I asked her how she liked the town but Ah! what do you think
She simply answered back again Oh! my but don't it stink.

188   *2 Feb 1906*

TO MY AULD BONNET

My guid auld frien' ye're gettin raggit
Though of your beauty ance I braggit
Ye're gettin holed and bare and scraggit
     Your linings gane
Wie grease and dirt ye're sairly claggit
     And mony a stain.

O' you I ance was prood and vaunty
And set ye on my heid sae jaunty
O' guid looks then ye warna scanty
     A thing of beauty
And tae admire ye there was plenty
     As 'twas their duty.

You're oft been mended stitched and patched
Wie cloots o' colour sair mismatched
When wearing you the stacks I've thatched
     For many a summer
And if ye now look sairly wratched
     'Deed tis na wunner.

Ye've been a shelter frae the wun'
A shade ye've been fra burning sun
When I've been oot wie rod or gun
     In leisure hoors
Or when wie hunds I took a run
     Across the moors.

Ye've kept me crannim nice and warm
And snug frae Winters snaw and harm
My brains oft worked like weel cork'd barm
    And many a sonnet
'Neath you's been hatch'd and oot did swarm
    My guid auld bonnet.

I've seen ye often brawly deckit
Wie bussy hooks that troots neglecit
Or some just new, frae dry gut neckit
    A thing perplexin
Whiles some guid flee by salmon wreckit
    Fair awfa' vexin.

And often when I went tae see
The lassie wie the glintin e'e
I wore ye then sae jauntily
    Set on three hairs
Or when I went wie mickle glee
    Tae shows or fairs.

I placed ye on me heid wie pride
That day I made me queen a bride
And ower the mountains sly did glide
    Tae Birdhope Craig
Then hameward Jean came by me side
    On shanky's nag.

Ye hae been put tae many uses
And suffered many sair abooses
The truth to tell I fear whiles looses
    In you hae jumpit
And often spiders webs frae hooses
    Wie you's been duntit.

Whiles when the guid wife had a cleckin'
And ither birdies were expeckin
In you she rowed them up I reckon
    Tae keep them warm

Time other anes their shells were breakin
    A' free frae harm.

And even this I maun alloo'
And when we rang the auld brood soo
    Her oft I grippit
Wie you and held her snooty mou'
    I case she slippit.

The auld hoose cat in you has kittled
The young whaulps oft in you hae pittled
And mony a time ye hae been bittled
    Across the green
When oft the bairnies played and scittled
    Some simmers e'en.

Ae time I'd been frae hame awa'
And left ye hingin on the wa'
When I cam' back a sight I saw
    You sair aboosed
The young deils kicked ye for a ba'
    Which made me roosed.

It happened ance we'd strangers got
And nae flesh meat tae boil the pot
Frae you the wife made fine stew hot
    Nice rich and greasy
And tae git a your strength I wot
    She sair did squeeze ye.

And though ye've suffered mony a slip
As oft's the case 'tween cup and lip
Yet always when the sheep we dip
    Nae ither bonnet
Sae weel as you I like tae slip
    My heid upon it.

When Winters tempests lood did bellow
When meads with buttercups were yellow
When Autumn fruits grew ripe and mellow

Aye on me heid
E'er since I was a shy young fellow
    Ye've been indeed.

Now guid auld frien' I've sung your praises
And though the fo'ks still at ye gazes
Its no ye'r beauty them amazes
Ye've nane ava
Ye're like your wearer full o'crazes
    Oor blooms awa'.

192   *No date*

TO MY GUID OLD TRUSTY FISHING ROD

My guid auld trusty fishing wand
Whene'er I get you in my hand
And hie off tae the rivers strand
    What hopes are mine
Nae other sport the test can stand
    Like joys o' thine.

Wie mony a fish we sair hae tussled
And aft the line through you has whussled
But though ye're sma' ye're right well muscled
    And winna break
While up and doon the saamon bustled
    For dear life's sake.

To many a jump and many a spang
Ye've proved yersel' baith brave and strang
The skirling reel aft sang a song
    Wie pure delight
As oot the line ran fast and lang
    Wie pith and might.

And when a fish had tired himsel'
Ye did your pairt then just as well
When near the shore they oft rebelled
    And ye get tested
Yet a' their strength at last ye quelled
    Them fairly bested.

But soon a'll hae to say ye by
My joints are gitten stiff and dry
I'm no sae gleg o' wrist and eye
    As I hae been
Old age and winter drawing nigh
    Will close the scene.

202   *12 March 1906*

TO MISS S. BELL. DACRE HOUSE, GILSLAND

Dearest Sallie I will rally
Up the fickle Muses
With heart contrite from them tonight
I will not take excuses
But first of all to you I shall
Express my obligation
And tender you, what is your due
My thanks and veneration.

On Saturday I'm glad to say
Your parcel came to hand
To say the least we had a feast
Fit for a lordly band
That young imp Jack his lips did smack
And rolled his eyes with pleasure
His buttons cracked his waistcoat racked
Beyond its usual measure.

In perfect health the greatest wealth
I'm' glad to say we're keeping
Except my thumb, which feels quite numb
And stops me much from sleeping
The truth to say the other day
A window I was closing
When down it came, with might and main
A broken rope disclosing.

Alas! for me that such should be
I thought my thumb was broken
The language used I fear abused
Had better not been spoken
Three nights I sighed and groaned and tried
To ease the pain relentless
But to my moans and outpoured groans
The Fates remained consentless.

But now today I'm glad to say
The pain hast much abated
This you may bet, I dont regret
But truly feel elated.
To this adieu I hope that you
Are keeping gay and cheerful
And by the shrine you do not pine
Of Cupid sad and tearful.

For I infer you yet prefer
Remaining free and single
And with a cat upon the mat
Sit by an old maids ingle
Perhaps you're right in case you might
Match with a hard taskmaster
As prudence bids steer clear of kids
And other such disaster.

A dreadful life has many a wife
No rest both night and day
The babe delights to scream at nights
And drives sweet sleep away

Or little Jane cries out with pain
And Tommy sets up squalling
While roused from sleep the husband deep
Pours forth his angry bawling.

In woeful plight all through the night
To save a household riot
She walks the floor 'twixt bed and door
To keep the baby quiet
Or if in bed she lays her head
The drowsy god imploring
She gets no rest as with great zest
Dear hubby takes to snoring.

When comes the morn unslept and worn
She has the fire to light
And spread the board at which her lord
In grumbling takes delight
With eggs and ham or bread and jam
He finds some fault or other
With angry looks he says none cooks
So well as did his mother.

She's bread to bake, and clothes to make
And do the household washing
And ah! how sad when hubby's mad
Perchance she gets a thrashing
Where is the bliss and lovers kiss
She once so fondly cherished
Alas they're gone and sad and lone
Her love's young dream has perished.

Now Cousin dear take warning here
Nor sigh at being single
For married life with care and strife
Doth very often mingle
Sweet Jeannie Moore will say I'm sure
Of sense the "poets" scanty
I'll married be if you keep free
And be the good old aunty'

I hope my Aunt of health's not scant
And that my Uncle dear
Keeps robust still nor dreads the ill
Of ever feeling "queer"
The clocks strikes ten I'll drop my pen
Nor Morpheous great repel
Be sure and write I'll say good-night
                    Yours ever
                         W. Bell.

207   *3 Apr 1906*

THE ROOKS

The rooks are flying round the trees
Amid the old plantation
And gathering sticks with which to fix
Their nesting habitation
With noisy caws and loud guffaws
There many a royal battle
Is sought and fought and brought to naught
O'er some high treasured wattle.

The husband goes to fetch a twig
While wife the nest is guarding
Lest some sly thief should work mischief
Their labours thus retarding.
Now on the nest they sit and rest
And chat about their labours
Or bold defy with angry cry
Their roguish thievish neighbours.

Now high above the wood they soar
In graceful circles wheeling
While from their throat escapes a note
Expressing wildest feeling

With pinions prest close to their breast
They drop with speed appalling
Then out each flings its glossy wings
Thus saving them from falling.

Both sly and crafty is the rook
And some name him a pest likewise
Yet he doth kill and eat his fill
Of grubs which bring our crops demise
If for his pains he gleans some grains
Perchance an odd potato
Let Nature be and you shall see
Her balance work first rate O!

209   *10 Apr 1906*

TOM ORD'S FAREWELL TO REDEWATER

Farewell to the vale of dear bonnie Redewater
Farewell to my friends aye so trusty and true
My tender heart bleeds when I think of the parting
And trembling my lips say their final adieu.

For eighty long years have my forbears lived in thee
And my old grannies eyes when one hundred years old
Were undimm'd as she gazed on the high lofty Carter
Where Phoebus sinks down in a pillar of gold.

Though often thy skies are frowning and clouded
And fiercely wild Boreas blows cold o'er thy fells
While ruthless the snowdrift careers o'er thy mountains
And thick the grey mists hug thy deep rocky dells.

Yet in Summer how fair are thy green emerald mountains
Where the young lambkins play by thy brooklets and braes
Whilst high in the awning the skylark sings sweetly
His paean of gladness of love and of praise.

Now the old farm steading lies deep in the deluge
And mournfully the waves sing a dirge as they roll
Yet more deep than the waters my burden of sorrow
And stronger the billows engulfing my soul.

But though I must leave thee thou dear peaceful valley
Yet near to my heart thou forever shalt be
And fondly I'll cherish wherever I wander
The sweet happy days that I have spent in thee.

Farewell to the vale of dear bonnie Redewater
Farewell to my friends aye so trusty and true
My tender heart bleeds when I think of the parting
And trembling my lips say their final adieu.

214   *May 1906*

TO SCOTIA FROM THE CARTER FELL

Scotia thy green hills and dales
Thy stately woods and rivers sweet
A simple bard with pleasure hails
And lays his tributes at thy feet.

Had I been reared in school or college
More ably could I sing thy praise
Alas! my head is scant of knowledge
And simple are my artless lays.

Yet all thy grandeur I admire
With all my heart I thee adore
And tune to thee my rustic lyre
Oh! would my song more sweet outpour.

Thou land whose heroes shed their blood
In freedom's cause their lives laid down
To stern oppressions mighty flood
They won themselves, and thee renown.

And still the martial spirit burns
Within the brave dear Scottish heart
Still she from base oppression turns
Aye ready to oppose its part.

Thy stalwart sons have climbed the heights
And honours won in every clime
With intellects all flashing bright
As diamonds from the deepest mine.

The mother thou of poets great
Who sweetly sang sublimest lays
Immortal their undying state
While Time shall weave his years from days.

O! Scotia fair, forever more
May Heaven guide thy destiny
Be thine the strong bow as of yore
Thine honour green as the bay tree.

219   *May 1906*

A CRACK WIE A COLLIE

Come awa' auld doggie
Let us hae a crack
While your maister's restin'
Sleepin' on his back
Man ye're lookin' tired
Puir auld faithful Sam
Ye'll no care how quickly
The last yowe dis lamb.

Come awa' auld doggie
Tell me all your woe
I see oft your maister
Hings his held gey low
Is your puir feet blistered
Man ye're getting' thin
Your auld banes are stickin'
Nearly through your skin.

Puir auld faithful doggie
Is your maister cross
Dis he ever at ye
His lang nibby toss
Dis he ever pelt ye
Wie sair hurtin' stanes
Say that if he catched ye
I break aw yer banes.

When things run on •smoothly
He'll no be sae bad
But when they're contrary
Then he will be mad
When a yowe is awkward
Ye'll get a' the blame
And he then will ca' ye
Mony a wicked name.

Puir auld faithful doggie
You're a useful beast
Is that some ane calling
Let us listen - wheest
Ah! it is your maister
He's whustlin' on you
Now again tis hill time
We mun say adieu.

TOM SAMSON

Tom Samson was a countryman
Just bordering on to fifty
A gayish dog he'd always been
And just a wee unthrifty.

He'd led a ranting roving life
And still a bachelor tarried
But now he thought 'twas time that he
Got settled down and married.

When first the thought had come to Tom
He fancied it a rum on'
As yet his mind was quite unfixed
Upon a likely woman.

But spurred by Cupid he looked round
Upon each maid and widow
And in the balance weighed each one
'Twixt Carter Fell and Skiddaw.

At last his mind was quite made up
He fixed upon a maiden
Who kept a little public house
Not very far from Blaydon.

She was not just a youthful maid
And often had been courted
Her age would just be forty-five
If truthfully reported.

When he had fixed upon his choice
Friend Thomas did not falter
But went at once to ask her if
She'd meet him at the altar.

His charmer did him well receive
With beaming smiling feature
And he unto himself declared
She was a lovely creature.

But when he reached the fatal point
He felt so very nervous
His only exclamation was
Heaven help us and preserve us.

But for his nervous bashful state
His idol did discover
An antidote that quickly soothed
Her nerve bestricken lover.

She poured him out a stiff strong glass
From a bottle standing handy
Of the good nectar Thomas loved
The very best pale brandy.

With courage filled up to the brim
By bold inspiring Bacchus
Tom clasped his charmer in his arms
And said love wilt thou tak'us.

The old maid blushed or tried to do
And whispered this is sudden
A speech that we may understand
Except our heads be wooden.

Tom pressed his suit with sentiment
As if he were demented
Then she did what she'd always meant
She kissed him and consented.

In three weeks time the marriage bells
Rang out their peals love laden
Whilst Thomas to the altar led
His buxom bride from Blaydon.

The honeymoon went quickly o'er
With many a blissful rapture
The bride thought that she surely had
Made a most lucky capture.

But very quickly she did find
Her spouse was fond of boozing
He'd sit up drinking late at night
Next morning he lay snoozing.

One day his wife did to him give
A task both grave and risky
She asked him to reduce for her
A bottle of proof whiskey.

Alas! temptation him beset
O'ercoming him with hauteur
He quickly drank up all the booze
But didn't touch the water.

Right speedily poor Tom became
With illness quite delirious
The doctor said his case at best
Was very grave and serious.

The stomach pump he used in vain
No strong emetic eased him
So quickly the hand of death
From all his trouble eased him.

Poor Thomas ne'er again will need
The tailor or the baker
A wooden suit for him was made
By Mister Undertaker.

ST. SWITHIN'S TEARS

Rain, rain, rain
Cloud and mist and vapour
Down from the hills come the angry rills
With many a jump and caper.

Grumble, grumble, grumble
The farmers tear their hair
While rumble, rumble, rumble,
The thunders rend the air.

Hay, hay, hay,
Why never a blessed ruck
But in the fields which abundance yields
It lies stinking and rotten as muck.

Lambs, lambs, lambs,
Here there is consolation
The only bright spot in the farmers lot
Amidst all the desolation.

Quack, quack, quack,
The ducks are active and happy
As they wander snailing, themselves regaling
With slugs both fat and sappy.

Fishermen, fishermen, fishermen,
All tell you the same merry story
For like to the duck the rain brings them luck
And they revel serene in their glory.

Weather, weather, weather,
The blessed thing's all gone to pot
The weather clerk's dead or else he has fled
To some more congenial spot.

TO A FRIEND ON HIS APPROACHING MARRIAGE

Od bliss us Johnny is it true
Ye'r really tae get wed sir
Unto a fine bit canty queen
Tae keep ye warm in bed sir.

Nae doot nae doot its shairly time
Ye're no just sic a chick sir
And many the lassies, faith its true
Ye lang hae been a brick sir.

O' hizzies big and hizzies sma'
Ye mony a ane did squeeze sir
I doot that ye hae been a man
That's unco bad tae please sir.

Ye've had them dark ye'd had them fair
Ye've had them auld and young sir
Some yibles that had nought tae say
And some gleg wie the tongue sir.

To choose a wife's a kittle job
As that ye maybe ken sir
There's guid and bad 'mang womankind
As weel as 'mang the men sir.

There's some tak's whiskey in their tea
And others like their beer sir
And some thats nane particular
When their guid man isna near sir.

Nae doot at first its unmixed bliss
Until the fun begins sir
Then when ye fetch the howdy wife
It maybe might be twins sir.

A sonsie laddie like yersel
A lassie like its mother sir
And while she dandles ae wee mite
Ye'll diddle tae the other sir.

And should the little dears at night
Scream lood and lang wie pain sir
Ye'll march the floor wie little Rob
The wife wie little Jane sir.

Should they be troubled with the gripes
The colic or the wind sir
Dill water, dose, a teaspoonful
Will blow it off behind sir.

But should it not bring them relief
To save you further toil sir
Them move their bowels and stop their howls
By cold drawn Castor Oil sir.

And if the little darling dears
Be loath to take the dose sir
Shove well the bottle down their throat
And grip them by the nose sir.

If in the morning you should rise
Your sark tail dripping wet sir
On marriet life ye'll ma'be look
A wee thought wie regret sir.

As aulder your dear bairnies grow
And show a temper wild sir
Remember he who spares the rod
Is apt to spoil the child sir.

If e'er the wifey should get cross
As whiles they shairly be sir
Then soothe her temper wie a kiss
And tak' her on your knee sir.

God bliss ye John my dear auld frien'
As well as your sweet lass sir
And when the wedding day comes off
Ye'll hae tae stand a glass sir.

But faith I doot sae wee a dram
Will hardly weet my throttle sir
A mans no marriet every day
We'd better ca'd a bottle sir.

And as I drink potations deep
They'll drive away my sorrow sir
With three times three my toast shall be
To you and Jeannie Murra' sir.

243   *No date   (1906)*

AN A'D MAID'S ADVENTURE AT BELLINGHAM SHOW IN
SEARCH OF A HUSBAND.

Aw am an a'd maid and my neums Mary Ann
And lang hev been on the leuk oot for a man
And aw'd oft heard it said if ye wanted a beau
The best place te git ane was Bellingham Show

Well a week past on Thursday, aw went tive the toon
And bought a new bonnet and a fine flash up goon
Ov the varry last fashion, begox they war stunning
Just like what the gentry aall wears up at Lon'non

The show mornin' arrived aw gat up wie the lark
And fixed on ma new dress aall up tive the mark
It had ta'en me two hoors when aw pat on ma bonnet
And aw'd sung ower a hundred times a loveladen sonnet.

As prood as a peacock aw leuked in the glass
Thinks aw but thou's not sic a bad looking lass
And certain aw feel that there's many a man
Would like to be mated with thee Mary Anne

To make a lang story short aw gat tive the show
And there aw began ma great quest for a beau
Aw thought it was best at the entrance to wait
To see all the men as they cam' through the gate

At th' exhibits to leuk aw felt not inclined
Something far mair important was searching ma mind
What the plague did aw care for a game cock or hen
Ma only great purpose was watching the men

Aw watched and aw waited till the toon clock struck three
Thinks aw Mary Ann its not aall gan to de
But just as ma hopes were beginnin' to sink
A chap cam' alang, and he gav' me a wink

He was drest up quite smart in a lood checkit coat
And wore a beard 'neath his jaw like a'd ' billy goat
A little wee mannie with his legs varry sma'
But his feet war the biggest that ever aw saw

He didn't leuk teakin as ma eyes did him scan
Thinks aw thou's no beauty but still thou's a man
Aw could see that the chep hed been hevin a glass
As he whispered begox but thou is a nice lass.

Ma heart fairly fluttered and gav' a great stoond
Thinks aw tive masel' that is Cupids awn wound
And when the man asked me aw couldn't say no
If aw wanted a sweetheart at Bellingham Show.

Aw linked ma hand through his airm in the a'd fashioned way
And aall over the showyard we happy did stray
Ma lover was talky and free wie his tin
He bowt me ma fairing of a chep ca'd Sam Quinn.

Now hinny he says we'll gan intiv the tent
Just to hev a wee toothful so aw gav' ma consent
With his airm roond ma waist, he stole a bit kiss
The forst time aw ever had tasted sic bliss

Aw tried hard to blush but aw didn't succeed
Now aall ye young lassies I pray you take heed
There's varry few women can say this wie me
That they'd never been kissed till they war' forty-three.

Now hinny he whispered what has to be thine
Will thou hev a small lemon or a drop sherry wine
Aw was kinda excited and it maybe was risky
But aw said aw wad just hev a small glass of whiskey

Of course I made faces like aall woman de
Except when they hev a drop on the Q.T.
Then they quick slip it ower wie a smack ov their lips
Oh! us women fooks aall are gay fond of wor nips.

Wor courtship in earnest now fairly began
A! thinks aw it's a nice thing to cuddle a man
Ma heid on his breast lay se nice and reposin'
Though aw thought that the chep was gay slow in proposin'.

An 'oor slipped away for old time will not wait
And we war just gan oot at the entrance gate
Suddenly ma lover turned aall queer and white
Just like tiv a man that hed gitten a fright

Aw looked around about me, and there aw saw cummin'
Takin' two steps at ance a great big fat a'd woman
She flew at ma lad wie a screetch and a yell
And brought doon on his poor heid her big umberel'.

For a second attack the poor chep didn't wait
But shot like an arrow right through the show gate
And ower by the brig he did quick steer his course
Wie the fire and mettle of a runaway horse.

Tiv me the a'd wife next turned her attention
And said sweery words that aw munnet here mention
But to sum up her story as short as aw can
She said that aw'd been trying to gan off wie her man.

Ye a'd bearded scorpion aw cried oot wie ire
That man is a ma sweetheart or else aw's a liar
Yer sweetheart she yells, O my but that's gran'
For twenty lang years aw've been wed to the man.

Aw was fairly dumbfoondered, what else could aw be
But aw telt the a'd wife she was telling a lee
Her eyes shone wie hate as her monkey arose
'Fore I knew what had happened she had twisted ma nose.

Cries aw ye a'd viper by some way or means
Its gay funny to me if ye divent get beans
So aw squared masel' up in the real proper style
While the crood gathered roond on their faces a smile.

At the varry furst meetin' away went ma bonnet
And the a'd hussy jumped wie her great feet upon it
Then next at ma hair, she made a great rive
Lord save us cries aw wad ye scalp me alive.

Disaster beset me again aw confess
Nearly torn from ma back was ma fancy new dress
Aw'd ne chance wie the a'd wife when we cam' into grips
She buttocked me clivor off her great fat big hips.

Thinks aw Mary Ann but this wark winnet de
If thou disn't de better it will soon be U.P.
It seems varry funny if thy wits cannot summon
A likely like plan for to punish that woman.

The great secret at last aw did solve in ma mind
Though as strong as Diana she was short of the wind
So aw dodged roond aboot her till aw gat her weel blown
Then aw had nae great doots but the day was ma own.

Tiv wark aw now gat, and the crood tiv a man
Yelled gan on the sma' ane, gan on Mary Ann
As aw planted them in on her big full moon face
In a scientific way as did great Johnny Mace.

Till aw catched her a ane beneath her fat chowks
That sent her eyes blinkin' like a pig wie the howks
Then aw quickly slipped in an a'd fashioned back heeler
The fall that she gat by the powers was a creeler.

A terrible great earthquake was felt in the North
Which shook aall the hills 'twixt the Humber and Forth
The fooks little thought as they ran to and fro
The cause of it aall was at Bellingham Show.

In the oor of ma victory aw heard a great crack
As something gav way in the sma' of ma back
'Twas them new fangled things wie the rosy cheek't neum
To call them owt else, wey aw fairly think shame.

And doon roond ma ankles they cam in due course
Aw was fairly weel hoopled like a Bos'ells fair horse
Aa kicked and a struggled 'twas all of ne use
The things wadn't tear nor and they wadn't come loose.

The men gav' three cheers and begox they war' ringers
While the bashful young lassies aall peeped through their fingers
As they watched how aw wriggled and capered aboot
Just like an a'd lord when he's mad wie the goot.

When the a'd wife leuked up and saw what was wrang
Like a mad raging lion upon me she sprang
She frothed at the mouth and excited did holler
While she squeezed oot ma life like a twenty ton roller.

Ther'd been murder committed, aw wad hev been killed
But providence kind had it otherwise willed
For up cam' two bobbies the disturbance to quell
And said that we'd baith hev tiv gan tiv the cell.

Says aw cannie cheps it's aall right thus to talk
But how the mischief d'ye think that aw's gannen to walk
So sergeant turned roond and spak' tiv his marra
Who quickly went off and cam' back wie a barrow.

Aw was placed in the bottom wie my legs tiv the front
The a'd wife on the hint end they quickly did munt
How the a'd huzzie shooted and loodly did squeal
As they placed her astride on a top of the wheel.

There was sic a procession as niver was seen
Ye'd have thought me a Duchess or even a Queen
There were motors and carriages and foot fook who ran
And shooted that's her that's gane daft for a man.

At last we arrived at the policeman's old hoose
And then ma poor ankles were quickly let loose
An angel of mercy was the sergeant's good wife
Who cut off ma hopples wie a big carving knife.

But what div ye think, od preserve us and bliss us
The young bobbie says Mary Ann will thou kiss us
Aw couldn't say no as ma case was so urgent
Aw gav' ane to the young chep and two tive the sergeant.

The let us baith oot just in time for the train
'Twas at the station aw saw my a'd sweetheart again
He was looking gey scared and white iv the mug
As his a'd mistress led him alang biv the lug.

Now aall you a'd maidens whate'r your degree
I hope you'll take warning by what befell me
Ye'd better bide single for that's no shame aw vo
Than seek for a husband at Bellingham Show.

A CRACK BETWEEN TWO BORDER SHEPHERDS

Upon a morn in early May
A cauld and sleety shoory day
Twa herds wie faces lang and sad
Each rowed up in a weel worn pla'd
Met on the stormy Cairter Fell
And sat them doon ahint a stell
Tae smoke their pipes and hae a blether
Aboot the lambing time and weather
And gie each other consolation
Amid sic awfa desolation.

The first that spak' his name was Bookie
He swore his verra tongue was yookie
Tae hae a lang and friendly talk
And unto Amos thus he spak'.

This weather man is most infernal
It bleeds ma heart right tae its kernal
There's no a blade o' gerse can growe
Tae bring the milk tae ony yowe
Jist cauld and slaistery sleety shoors
And frosty through the midnight oors
There's no a blink o' welcome sun
And sic a cauldrife biting wun'
How's your things daeing man ava
We've oft been happit up wie snaw.

Then Wollie Amos grew quite talky
As he cut off a pipe o' baccy
He drew his plaid oot ower his heid
And says O verra bad indeed
Ma guid auld frien' and neebor Bookie
I'll bet wie you a Jethert Cookie
And your chance man's as sma' tae win it
As there'll be straggling curnies in it.

There's no a herd hed sic a time
In Coquet water Reed or Tyne
As aw hev hed this last fortnight
Od bliss us man aw'm nearly gite
What wie ae thing and another
Ma mind hes oft been in a swother
Whether life was worth the leevin
When its sae filled wie strife and grievin
Nae fether gane than yester morn
Od man but aw could fairly sworn
Ma best pack yowe was lying awled
Wie louping ill anither sprawled
Six bonnie lambs that weel aw cherished
War lying lifeless cauld and perished

The gimmer wie the shed ram tippit
Twa rotten lambs tae me hed slippit
And yon nice hogg that weel ye worded
Was reeling roond aboot and sturdied
Ma auld bitch Queen had gane and whelpit
Ma young dog wie distemper yelpit
Od man ma life is waur than hell
Aw hae tae rin and bark masel'.
Ye maybe think that this is plenty
But aw'm no dune sae neebor tent ye
At denner time aw gaed the byre
A cow was smitten wie a clyre
Ower at the stye the pig was screaming
Thinks aw the beast is mad a breeming
But when aw lookit ower the door
Aw plainly saw 'twas something wor'
It stood and snorkit blew and wheezled
Thinks aw the beast is shairly measled
Wie Castor Oil aw weel did doose her
But naething seemed ava tae roose her
This morning (here he shook his heid)
The puir bit beast was lying deid.
And noo ma verra heart is breakin
Tae think aw've lost sae muckle bacon.

Lord bliss us man cried bookie Bill
For thirty year a've climbed this hill
And neebor them that's been a fore ye
Ne'er telt me sic a mournful story
But ma auld cock lot me you tell
There's mae hes trouble than yoursel'
In this world we a' get oor share
And faith there's some gets even mair.
Ye mind yon guild show vow o' mine
The best in Coquet Reed or Tyne
Her that aw hed at Elliot's ram
Aw thought she hae a bonnie lamb
But man aw hae been sair mistean
Aw never frien' saw sic weean'
Nae bigger than a full grown stoat
And just as hairy as a goat
Ma auldest son (ye ken oor Willie)
Says its been gotten wie a billy.
And man ye'll mind yon bonnie gimmer
Ye saw when ye war' o'er a simmer
The best sheep aw hed on ma hill
Od Sir but she hes paid me ill.
Then Bookie seized his lambing nibby
And waved aloft its weel turned gibby
And doon it cam' on his sho' nebs
The clairty beast hes cussen kebs
And O ma heart has got a stoond
This morning she was lying drooned

Away ayont the Colliers pike
In a deep hole in Drumlie Syke.
And now a've naething left tae lick
The sheep o' Watty o' the Nick.
The ither morn we'd sic a rowdy
The wife cried oot send for the howdy
And rin yersel' like ony negger
And hurry on the wee McGregor
Man wad'en ye hae thought the hizzie

'Ood hed mair sence and us sae buisy
However on ma job aw went
And soon wie rinning was fair spent
But Fortune favours aye the brave
Between the cradle and the grave.
Aw met oor mutual frien' auld Robbie
Wha munted on his mear sae nobby
And doon the Jed did quickly gallop
His legs and airms gan wallop wallop

Ye're speiring what the youngster be
Lord bliss ye man but there are three
Twa bonnie lassies and a laddie
A' to be rowed up in ma pladdie.

Says Amos frien' we'll hae tae gang
Oor time is short oor journeys lang
Aw'll see ye on the great occasion
Ye're comin' tae the valuation.

Withoot a doot cries oot brave Bookie
There's waur things than cauld roasted chookie
And to cure care and mak' us frisky
Commend me tae a wee drap whiskey.

Then cam' a great black sleety shoor
At which they baith looked grin and dour
And each his pla'd aboot aim rowes
And spanks away across the knowes.

(A howdy is a midwife)

TO SEE THE KING AT ALNWICK

Twas in the month of fair July
The sun was shining in the sky
As Charlie and his mates did hie
Tae see the King at Alnwick.

As they were marching up the street
A kingly form them a' did greet
The verra man we cam' tae meet
They joyfully cried at Alnwick.

I am the king withoot a doot
But dinna let the secret oot
Or else there will be sic' a shoot
As ne'er was heard in Alnwick.

But gie us a bit wag o' your han'
How's a' wi'e on the Borderlan'
Now ye will hae the drinks tae stan1
Since we hae met at Alnwick.

My lord my liege and faith we will
Now will ye tak' a gless or gill
Oh! just a drap fra Reekie's still
Since we hae met at Alnwick.

Its prime, its prime, then cries the king
Now ye tae me a sang mun sing
And then we'll dance the Heilin fling
Since we're a' met at Alnwick.

Young Charlie stood wie open mooth
An' says now Edward quench your drooth
How are things lookin' far up Sooth
When ye left hame for Alnwick.

The tattie craps are lookin' weel
The turnips a' met i' the driel
They'll be nae scarcity o' meal
I prophecy at Alnwick.

Noo as tae me ye hae been kin'
Yell tak' a single glass o' mine
The verra best o' vinted vine
That ever was in Alnwick.

He drew a bottle frae his pooch
This is the best as I can vooch
Now tak' yourselves a good big slooch
An' drink my health in Alnwick.

Each fellow drained his sparkling glass
What after that there cam' tae pass
They never knew for Ah! Alas
They senceless lay at Alnwick.

But when they a' cam tae theirsel'
Each purse was gane each watch as well
An' they war a' locked in a cell
Within the toon o' Alnwick.

And deil a king they'd ever seen
Nor had they lookit on the Queen
Aw doot oor frien's mun hae been green
Amang the prigs at Alnwick.

Now they did mournfully moan and wail
Nae frien's had they to stan' their bail
They're doing now a month in jail
A' ower their ploy at Alnwick.

What fun they'll be when they come hame
A word o' this we'll no dar' name
Aw doot they'll ne'er gang back again
To see the King at Alnwick.

OLD FARMER BROWN

Old Farmer Brown from Hayspoil town
Looks from his window with a frown
To see the rain come pouring down
  Upon his hay
Where in the fields it lies quite brown
  From day to day.

His face looks weary and dejected
His hair is long, his beard neglected
He long stern ruin has expected
  But now at last
By his strong grip he is infected
  All hope is past.

He bites his nails then tears his hair
And loud and wrathfully doth swear
Anon he offers up a prayer
  To Heaven
That but three weeks of weather fair
  To him be given.

He thumps his glass upon the wall
But it will only drop and fall
Then forth he stalks out of his hall
  To view the skies
Where only clouds hang like a pall
  Before his eyes.

The servant men about the place
The days disasters well can trace
As they gaze on his clouded face
  And quick retire
To make hay ropes where there is space
  In shed or byre.

When Tom the herd comes from the fell
With some dark dismal tale to tell
How some good ewe by syke or stell
    Is dead or dying
Then nothing can his spleen repel
    Or satisfy him.

His thrifty careful loving wife
Has now a dreary doleful life
Her lot is filled with naught but strife
    Both night and morn
While at her heart she feels the knife
    Of hubby's scorn.

When she with him tries to condole
He pulls a face would spane a foal
And sends her to Old Satan's hole
    With bristling ire
Where they need neither wood nor coal
    To light a fire.

When his old dog his hand doth lick
He gives the faithful beast a kick
Or on his back brings down his stick
    Hard as he can
Of sympathy he's heartly sick
    From beast and man.

When forth he goes to Mart or Fair
And meets his brother farmers there
Then lamentations rend the air
    Both loud and deep
While with potations they drown care
    And talk of sheep.

Awhile he will forget his care
Awhile will Fortunes face look fair
While Bacchus bears his willing share
    Without a frown
Yet of him you had best beware
    Old Farmer Brown.

TAMMY HEESLOP'S MUSINGS AT THE PEAT STACK END

Ma neum is Tammy Heeslop
Aw am a shepherd laddie
Ma faither hails frae Copshawholm
Ma mither frae Kirkca'dy.

We live far oot amang the hills
And nae doot this is awkward
And whiles aw think aw maybe am
A wee thowt shy and backward.

A' through the year we're maistly fed
On tattie stew and brawxy
But at the best aw must confess
Its raither tough and waxy.

But noo we have a welcome change
Oor weams are right weel rackit
There's meat and plenty in the burn
Though its a risk tae tak'it.

Though why it should be puzzles me
And what aw'd like tae mention
Wha ever made the fishing laws
Bad luck tae their invention.

The fish were shairly made for man
At least thats ma opinion
Else why were they from time remote
Placed 'neath his great dominion.

But grasping lairds have made their laws
Wie deevilish invention
And made them jist tae suit themselves
Whate'er be their pretention.

The ither day doon at the lynn
A lot o' fish were jumpin'
As shair as deith aw was na lang
A muckle big ane gumpin'.

Next day we tarred some auld meal pokes
A' ready tae be lighted
No' that night but the next again
The saumon could be sighted.

Oor Jock and me tied on oor cleeks
Ma faither shanked his leister
And soon we gat as many fish
As will ser' us till Easter.

When we gat hame my mother had
Upon the fire the yetling
And wasna lang a right guid feed
O' saumon for us fettling.

We cleaned and sauted a' the rest
And packed them in a ferkin
And covered them a' snugly up
Wie faithers auld worn jerkin.

We hid them shall I tell you where
Aw see your een are glistening
But let me whisper in your lug
Lest Abraham be listening.

For if he should find oot the place
Ma word we should be shakin'
We'd hae tae pay the piper dear
Or in the jail lie quakin'.

Oor watchers are sic cunning men
Gan creepin' on their hunkers
Aye on the look for luckless herds
Or less experienced younkers.

But though they be baith gleg and sly
They canna aye be watchin'
And theres nae sin the deil a grain
Yersel' a saumon catchin'.

But if ye will tak' ma advice
Ye'd better jist be cautious
For if ye're catched ye'll find the job
Expensive is and fashious.

And though awm but a country lad
No' blest wie muckle learning
The virtue o' oor fishing laws
Is 'yont ma poor discerning.

252   *27 Nov   1906*

AN UP TO DATE LOCINVAR

Oh! the young Locinvar has crossed over the Forth
From the land of the Tartan that lies in the North
Right down from the Highlands he motored alone
O'er roads smooth and even, o'er roads rough with stone
O'er pavements of wood and macadam of tar
Like a flash of fleet lightening came young Locinvar.

Past town and past village he stayed not his pace
But madly kept on as if bent on a race
Through a great flock of sheep he careered like the wind
Leaving stones of good mutton bestrewn behind
He heard not the shouts of the shepherds afar
As reviling they called on the young Locinvar.

Six bullocks he slaughtered two pigs and a hen
Two horses a donkey and a score of good men
Ten dear ladies fainted as they saw him rush past
While those left unharmed stood with faces aghast

But he heeded them not as he sang a sweet bar
Light hearted and happy felt young Locinvar.

Six police who tried to stay his mad pace
Serenely he passed with a smile on his face
While three of these worthies lay gasping and prone
He gaily went on with his number unknown
Each rose from the ground with a deep bleeding scar
And cursed that mad demon the young Locinvar.

But at last in descending a steep rugged hill
Our hero encountered a mighty great spill
The brakes refused action he struck the road fence
His body flew forward his spirit went hence
Next morning were found neath the upturned car
The mangled remains of the young Locinvar.

Now all who drive motors a lessen here learn
You yet the respect of the public may earn
Don't scorch o'er the road like mad demons let loose
As if it had solely been made for your use
Drive careful and steady 'tis better by far
Than to share the sad fate of the young Locinvar.

256   *10 Nov   1906*

FALLING LEAVES

One by one the leaves are falling
From the fast denuding tress
One by one they fall and scatter
In the chilly Autumn breeze.

One by one the leaves are falling
Yellow, crimson, brown and gold
Dead and dying Summers tributes
That it pleased us to behold.

One by one the leaves are falling
Leaving sprig and branches bare
Which the woodland nymphs in grandeur
Richly decked with lavish care.

One by one the leaves are falling
And they whisper as they fly
Of the waning year that's hastening
On the time we too must die.

One by one the leaves are falling
One by one we mortals fall
Leaves and lives by Times strong breezes
Wafted far beyond recall.

261   *1906*

A CHRISTMAS GREETING TO FRIENDS AT WILLINGTON ON
TYNE

My dearest friends at Number five
I hope that you are all alive
And hearty happy gleg and croose
And able to devour this goose.
But maybe frae the truth I wander
Wha kens but it might be a gander
But what e'er be its name or gender
I hope you'll find it sweet and tender.

And that it pleasure will afford
As you sit round your Christmas Board
Each one with happy smiling face
And after Paters said the grace
He'll seize upon the carving knife
And first of a' he'll help "the wife"

118

A guid big shive frae aff the briest
No' less than half a pund a least

Then maybe it might be as well
Though impolite tae help himsel'
In case he might be sair neglockit
Before he gets it a' disseckit
Then next tae my auld cronie Meg
He'll scollop aff the left hint leg
And then in case of a dilemma
He'll gie its walking mate tae Emma

Tae Jackie Bell the verra thing
Will be the birdie's right hand wing
And then withoot a stop or swother
He'll whussle aff tae Nance the other.
Next unto Hannah he will whack
A guid big dad frae off the back
And unto Tam the Rosehill wizard
He'll gie the thrapple and the gizzard

A tasty bites still left for Rab
He'll get the stamach and the gab
And tae my rhyming brither Jack
He'll quickly pass the banes tae crack
But jist in case the Bard we're huffin
Gie him an extra lump o' stuffin'
And after ye've a' had your fill
Ye each will tak' a Beechams Pill

For 'tis a fact beyond a' question
They powerfully aid and help digestion
On second thoughts it might save trouble
If ye gie Meg a dose thats double.

Now ma poor Muse aw menna worry
Nor work her up into a flurry
For she's a jad' tae be respeckit
No' worked ower hard nor yet neglockit

So aw will bid ye a' guid night
And with a heart leal and contrite
Wish ane and a' baith lad and lass
A happy jovil bright Christmas.

269   *19 Dec   1906*

WEARY WILLIE

O! weary Willie is a man
We're very often meeting
A dirty blanket and a can
His worldly goods completing
He trudges on along the roads
Yet never in a hurry
A crust he finds when hunger goads
And never needs to worry.

With battered hat all rent and torn
A coat and waistcoat raggy
With matted hair and beard unshorn
And nether garments baggy
His shoes are cut and freely gashed
To ease his blistered toes
And his black sooty face unwashed
No soap nor water knows.

Poor Willie is a man I fear
Who isn't much admired
To most of people it is clear
That he was born tired
He feels incapable of work
He knows a game much better
That is to prowl around and lurk
Without a binding fetter.

Yet Willie always gets his grub
Hip pipe he smokes with pleasure
And should he get reproof or snub
He takes such at his leisure
In Summer when the sun shines bright
He basks himself and snoozes
While dreaming dreams of glad delight
And doing as he chooses.

Then at the closing of the day
Will never seeks a skipper
Snug in some pike of new won hay
Reposes this gay tripper
Next morning from the field he steals
Before appears the farmer
When Sol his cheery face reveals
And makes the air feel warmer.

Sometimes when Willie's feeling fit
He takes to catching vermin
And in some private place he'll sit
His unwashed shirt discernin'
And when he spies a sprightly louse
Inactive he'll not linger
But with alertness born of use
Cracks it 'twix thumb and finger.

If at a public house he meet
Another brother Weary
Then these two worthies each stand treat
And speedily grow cheery
With secret confidential talk
While they their pints are tossing
They tell of where theres grub to stalk
And of convenient dossing.

His maxim always seems to be
I'll have a life thats easy
And to work off his energy

He mates a wife as greasy
But the sly rascal very soon
Will play the gay deceiver
And after a short honeymoon
He'll take the road and leave her.

But when comes Winter cold and grey
Poor Will does shake and shiver
And to the workhouse wends his way
With an inactive liver
Perchance within his frame are sown
The seeds of fell bronchitis
Or since it has the fashion grown
Dies of Appendicitis.

Then he's laid in a paupers grave
Where he sleeps on quite soundly
To work he never was a slave
But here he rests profoundly
And if his epitaph you'd write
Above his grave so chilly
You truly may therein indite
Unwept is Weary Willie.

271   *25 Dec 1906*

WINTER (2)

The wintry wind is howling
The earth with snow is white
The leaden skies are scowling
A dreary joyless sight
The trees all bare and leafless
The flowers all dead and gone
The songbirds mute and silent
Sit pensive sad and lone.

The robin seeks the barnyard
The partridge haunts the green
The hare when falls the gloaming
Slips to the fields unseen
Upon the patch of turnips
To make her evening meal
The greedy rooks and jackdaws
The pinch of hunger feel.

The mountain sheep are gathered
Around the sheltering stells
The Jack Snipe now frequenteth
The frost resisting wells
The wild geese flying southwards
All telling the same tale
That all around relentless
Cold Winter doth prevail.

O! Winter cold stern Winter
Though thou be strong and bold
We care not for thy coming
Much rather we'd behold
The earth and woods resplendent
Bedecked with leaves and flowers
And Nature all rejoicing
In Summers gladsome hours.

276   *23 Jan 1907*

TORMENTS OF SCIATICA

What is that awfa' pain I feel
That gars me grane and girn and squeel
That doon ma leg does tearing steal
    Wie lightening flash
Then up again wie sudden wheel
    Does madly dash.

First in my back it gies a nip
Then through my haunch wie raging rip
Then doon my leg it gies me jip
  To you I vow
Fast ower my face the sweat does trip
  Frae aff my brow.

The toothake is a savage pain
When it does rage wie might and main
But even it I'd raither gain
  Than suffer this
Ay twenty times I see it plain
  It wad be bliss.

The Doctors gie me nasty stuff
At which my stamach takes the huff
Anithor lot teemed in ma loof
  Tae weel rub in
That quickly raises a' the scruff
  Frae aff my skin.

But plague a bit o' ease they bring
My face looks dour my heid aw hing
And when in bed the claes I fling
  And whiles I fear
I may let slip that wicked thing
  Folks ca's a swear.

There is an awfa' place o' woe
Where a' tormented spirits go
But faith I think if doon below
  Is waur than this
I'll try the very best I know
  That place tae miss.

TO ROBIN AT THE WINDOW

Little robin, little robin,
Now that Winter's come again
And the dreary winds are sobbing
Thou comest knocking at my pane
So I gently raise the window
And thou'rt welcome to come in
To refuse thee room and shelter
Little bird would be a sin.

Little robin, little robin,
So in at last thou'rt come
And thy little heart is throbbing
As thou pickest up a crumb
Fain, fain would I caress thee
But I know that should I try
Thou would'st spread thy airy pinions
And away again would'st fly.

Little robin, little robin,
Where sleep'st thou midst the storm
But then it takes so little
To shelter thy wee form
And thou'rt snugly covered over
With a downy feathered coat
And always hast a fire
All aglow around thy throat.

Little robin, little robin,
Soon the winter day will fly
Then again into the greenwood
A wooing thou wilt hie
And when at last thou'rt mated
Thou will build thy little nest
And soon with joys maternal
Shall throb thy scarlet breast.

Little robin, little robin.
There is One who cares for thee
He who placed thee in the forest
To a life forever free
And though dear little robin
Thy lot be very small
Yet the wise and good Creator
Loves, guards, and watches all.

284   *18 Mar 1907*

THE ANVIL OF VULCAN IS SILENT TODAY
<u>Lines on the tragic death of Robert Ormiston Elsdon</u>

In the lone vale of Redesdale, hangs a dark cloud of sorrow
And each heart has been touched, with the blight of dismay
There is weeping and wailing and sadness prevailing
O'er the Anvil of Vulcan, so silent today.

In the prime of young manhood, so sudden and tragic
Came that stern call, we would fain disobey
Though we be consentless, yet death is relentless
And the Anvil of Vulcan is silent today.

No more from his anvil we'll watch the sparks flying
As we gather around on the cold Winter's day
His work is relinquished, his fire extinguished
His Anvil forsaken and silent today.

Blow, blow ye wild winds o'er the steep rugged mountains
And let your sad dirges their comfort convey
To our hearts as they languish in sorrow and anguish
O'er the Anvil of Vulcan so silent today.

Yet amidst our dejection, amidst our deep sorrow
Hope pinions her flight to fair regions away
Where father and mother and sister and brother
Shall meet him whose Anvil is silent today.

PATES HAMECOMING FRAE OTTERBURN BALL

One wintry morn the clock struck four
When someone knocked upon my door
In haste I sprang unto the floor
    Put on my breeks
And through the window to explore
    I slyly keeks.

But no one could my eyes espy
Who's there, I sleepily did cry
When from below came this reply
    In voice forlorn
Oh! let me in or I shall die
    This winters morn.

Ye ken me weel ma name is Pate
Who lives up in the watergate
Od man aw am in sic' a state
    Jist fairly din
Ye'll maybe think that I'm no blate
    But lets be in.

Another tick I didna waste
But doon the stairs I came in haste
Opened the door, when like a ghaist
    Wie hingin heid
Slowly across the threshold paced
    A man near deid.

Od man says he I'm fair forgoughen
Wie that strang wun I ha' been duffin
Im oot o' breath and blawn and puffin
    Ma empty kite
Wad mickle better be o' stuffin'
    Its toom and light.

So up the fire I quickly roosed
While Peter graned and snored and snoozed
I plainly saw the chap was boosed
    While there he sat
Heid on his hands right weel ramfoosed
    He bowked and spat.

Says I now Peter my guid frien'
Ye'll shairly tell me where you've been
Nae doot wie some fine buxom queen
    Ye hae been sportin'
Na, na, cries he wie doleful mein
    I've no been courtin.

Tae tell a lie man I wad spurn
Last night my fancy took a turn
Tae gang doon tae Otterburn
    Unto the ball
But there again I'll ne'er sojourn
    I never shall.

Wie cleecking reeling and advancing
Wie jumping caperin' and sic' dancing
'Many lassies glorious and entrancing
    I spent the night
And draps o' whusky sent me prancing
    And filled me tight.

At twa oclock my bike astride
I started on my hameward ride
And speedily I thowt I'd glide
    Up through the glen
But we ne'er ken what woes betide
    The sons of men.

Ma poor auld guts gangs jiggle jog
As empty as a sair rushed hogg
Tae step across a drain or bog
    O' ony length

I'll hae tae gang on seeds or fog
Tae gie me .strength.

But O I wadna' cared a fraction
If I'd no' broke our friendly paction
And left ahint my ain mate Jackson
It is nae fable
He's lying drunk, clean oot o' action
In Posty's stable.

Says I the morn he will be dry
And have a bleary bloodshot eye
Cries Pate he's better off than I
He'll tak' nae ill
For snugly in his arms dis lie
A full three gill.

Nae doot now Peter my guid man
Amang the jads ye'd try your han;
You bet says he I worked the plan
Up tae the nine
A braw young lass ye'll understan'
Said she'd be mine.

As nice and fine a strappin' queen
As ever on I clappit een
Just bordering unto seeventeen
Wie cheeks sae rosy
Fresh as the dew bespangled green
A regular posey.

I made a promise honour bright
To meet wie her on Sunday night
But man when fooks are kinda tight
They promise then
Things they'll no dae, yet maybe might
Ye ken, ye ken.

A pund o' beef steak I did fry him
A pint o' tea I set close by him

Wie dads o' bread tae satisfy him
> Then by the fire
Wie satisfaction I did eye him
> Whose waem rose higher.

The pint o' tea he quickly suppit
The beef steaks into him he whuppit
His neive the empty pot then gruppit
> Fill that again
My faith says he I was fair stupit
> Wie hungers pain.

I sat and watched in silence dumb
And eyed Pates waem rise like a drum
Sine tae himsel a tune he'd hum
> Some Irish jig
Than tae the fireside he did come
> Blawn oot and trig.

Od man says he I better feel
Sin' I gat that into my creel
I'm fit again tae dance a reel
> Hev ye a fiddle
Oh never mind, 'twill dae as weel
> If ye will diddle.

A merry tune tae him I whussled
While on the floor he lap and bussled
His legs sae soople and untrussled
> Few could him bate
A clean baned lad and right weel muscled
> Nae doot is Pate.

At last the day began to break
When hameward he his way did take
He gaed me a right hearty shake
> O' his strung han'
Saying keep this mum for ony sake
> Ye understan'.

Oh! hae nae fear I'll keep it quiet
Lest it should raise a wordy riot
Ye'll fin' I am nae noisy pi'ot
	Tae clash and chatter
Nae cause ye'll have frae me tae sigh at
	Sae end the matter.

But faith its ower guid tae keep
And though it makes our hero weep
To you in confidence I cheep
	This truthful tale
And lang may Peter tend his sheep
	O'er moor and dale.

288   *6 Mar 1907*

SINCE GEORDIE TEUK ON TO THE BEER

When forst aw got wed tiv wor Geordie
Aw thowt aw hed got a gud man
And we war' as happy as could be
Until he his drinking began
But now aw am sair broken hearted
And hev been for mony a year
Though Geordie is not a bad husband
Except when he gits on the beer.

When forst aw gat wed we'd a cottage
All furnished se neatly and trim
And the sunshine ov life was wor Geordie
So fondly aw doted on him
He browt me hame regular his wages
And of trouble aw hedn't a fear
But O! how things sairly hev altered
Sin' Geordie teuk on tiv the beer.

The bairns war all joyous and happy
When Geordie cam hame ov a night
And clasped in his airms the young infant
Crooed laughed and did jump wie delight
But now they creep intiv a corner
Not a word frae their lips div aw hear
They knaw varry weel te keep quiet
When Geordie comes hame on the beer.

Their claes are sair tattered and raggit
And shoes tiv their feet they hev nane
The varra bit blankets tae hap them
Te the pawnshop their faither hes ta'en
Wie hunger they often are greetin
That breaks ma poor heart for to hear •
'Twas an awful bad job for wor bairnies
When Geordie teuk on tiv the beer.

Wor hoose now leuks cheerless and empty
The things hev all gane to buy bread
And on some ad rags in the corner
We have to make nightly wor bed
Geordie sometimes that badly dis use me
Oot o' doors aw'm ashamed tiv appear
O! a pityful life hes a woman
When her husband takes on tiv the beer.

O! if only he wad stop his drinking
We even yet happy might be
For a gud loving wife and a helpmate
He'd willingly still find in me
If it hedn't been for the bit bairnies
Aw wad welcome the grave chill and drear
And yit Geordie is not a bad husband
Except when he gits on the beer.

THE DOOSING O' THE HOGGS

The Back End again is with us,
The wun blaws cauld and chill
And nightly hoarfrost's whiten
Each valley, and each hill
The moorland herds are at it
Wie their useful collie dogs
Busy pairting and ashedding
For the doosing o' the hoggs.

Auld Grumphie has been dieted
On new cow milk and grass,
Her dung collected and stirred up
Into a sickly mass
A glassful doon each throat is teemed
Then oot into the fogs
For four and twenty hours completes
The doosing o' the hoggs.

I spiered o' my frien' Danny
And I spiered o' John and Nick
And each declared for "seekness"
'Twas a glorious specific
But Wullie o' the Seven Sykes
Says he will bet his cloggs
'Tis just an auld wife's fancy,
Is the doosing o' the hoggs.

Says I ye shairly dinna think
It dis nae guid ava
Last year says he wie doosing them
I had an awfa' fa'
Next morn I'd fifteen lying deid
As cauld and stiff as logs
Na, na, says he I'll no' believe
In doosing o' the hoggs.

Some will express nae opinion.
But like a' cautious men,
Just shake their heids wie solemn look,
And say they dinna ken,
But though they silent be and deep
As ony mossy bogs
They'll hae their ain bit fancies
On the doosing o' the hoggs.

Wie opinions sae divided
What has ane tae believe
If we doose them they may seeken
If we dinna we may grieve
Thus muses mony an auld herd
As through his flock he jogs
Its a kind o' kittle subject
Is the doosing o' the hoggs.

(Hoggs are lambs that have been weaned but not yet (usually) mated)

308   *No Date*

THE PLUCKING O' THE GEESE

Around the kitchen they did sit,
Each bonnie lass and lad,
And every face did wear a smile
And every heart felt glad,
So quickly each ane grippit tight
A feathered bird a piece
For they had met the night tae spend
At the plucking o' the geese.

As Wullie tore the feathers off,
An auld grey goose's leg,
Losh sake cries he I'll bet ma breeks
This is an ancient stegg.

134

It seems tae me its shairly had
O' life a gey lang lease,
But we had better keep that dark,
At the plucking o' the geese.

But Johnnie was a canty chiel,
Wha dearly loved a lark,
Says he auld frien' thats just the bird
That kekkled in the Ark
Frae him and his auld mate lang gane
He's seen his kind increase
Nae wonder that he's raither tough
At the plucking o' the geese.

The matrimonial news went roond
Each little tittle tat
How Neddy Johnson lang had been
Amang the queens a flat
But how at last he had got wed
Unto the Majors niece
And that was how the crack went roond
At the plucking o' the geese.

They talked aboot their neebour herds
Wha flittin' were in swarms
How Wull and Jock and Rab and Tam
Were hunting after farms
How Sandy's best shed Cheviot tip
Was harshish o' the fleece
And that was how the crack went roond
At the plucking o' the geese.

The auld wife sat sae cooth and snug
And joined them in their crack
Sine said now bairns its shairly time
That ye should hae a snack
The dainty table soon was spread
Frae toil they found release
And a right good royal feast had they
At the plucking of the geese.

Now after they'd a' had their fill
Tam's fiddle it did squeel
And ilka lad and ilka lass
Joined in a lightsome real
The midnight hour went quickly by
The fun did never cease
And guileless pressure reigned that night
At the plucking of the geese.

The melodian young Matty squeezed
And Johnnie sang a sang
While Robbie danced the Hielan' fling
Wie many a loup and spang
And ever since that happy night
Sweet Aggie's had nae peace
When Isaac stole away her heart
At the plucking of the geese.

Then here's tae a' the shepherd men
That spank across the knowes
May loupin' ill ne'er carry off
Their lambies or their yowes
May seekness braxy or the like
Their hoggies ne'er decrease
And many a happy night be theirs
At the plucking of the geese.

319   *31 Dec 1908*

HEV' YE IVER BEEN AT ELSDON

Hev ye iver been at Elsdon
That village of renown
It stands amid the heathy hills
Which often wear a frown
Hev ye iver been at Elsdon

Its gitten a bad neum
But the folk that libel Elsdon
Foriver should think sheum.

Hev ye iver been at Elsdon
Tis often aw've been there
And even man at Elsdon
Aw've dined on kingly fare
They div'nt feed on heather broth
Nor yit on peesweep eggs
Nor even on an Irish stew
Made oot o' deein' steggs.

Hev ye iver been at Elsdon
Oh! how ma heart dis throb
When aw think on that happy day
Aw spent wie keeper Bob
And other friends at Elsdon
Within the Blackbirds Nest
Where there are viands sumptuous
And wassail of the best.

Hev ye iver been at Elsdon
Oh! weel aw mind the night
Aw slept sae snug at Elsdon
'Mid blankets clean and white
They hev ne buggs at Elsdon
And neither lice nor fleas
So ye can sleep at Elsdon
As happy as ye please.

Hev ye iver been at Elsdon
Just listen what says "Whist"
There's sweetest maids in Elsdon
A' waiting to be kissed
The best coal come frae Elsdon
The varry best o' beef
And ne'er a man in Elsdon
That ye could ca' a thief,

If ye've niver been at Elsdon
Take ma advice and gan
For ivery chiel in Elsdon
Is ivery inch a man
Ay there's decent folks in Elsdon
As iver aw did see
So aw'm away to Elsdon
And come alang wie me.

335   *1914*

SIGNS OF SPRING

There are crocus blooms in the garden,
There's a patch of blue in the sky,
There's a skylark sweetly singing
As he wings his way on high.

There's a silver gleam on the river,
There's a wagtail near the door
There's a dipper's nest a-building
Where there's oft been one before.

There are forming buds in the forest
There's a ribbon of green on the fell
There are blackbirds busy courting
In loves old way in the dell.

There's a call to awake from slumber
There's an end to dark winter's dreams
There's a rubbing of eyes and a blinking
To the glare of Sol's fitful beams.

There's a Springtide drawing nearer
So youthful and full of grace
And we'll welcome the love and laughter
Portrayed on her smiling face.

336 *Mar 1917*

SNOWBOUND TRAVELLERS
See Chapter 5 p152: Fred Terry's encounter with Billy Bell

337 *No date*

LINES ATTACHED TO A HIDDEN BICYCLE

Oh had I been a wicked thief
Your bike might have stolen
And left you with long miles to tramp
With feet and ankles swollen
So just in case that I should fall
Beneath some great temptation
Please hide it in another place
Upon the next occasion.

341 *No Date(1917 ?)*

WINTER ON THE CARTER FELL.

Oh! its dour and snell on the Carter Fell
On a cauldrife winters morning
When the sna' lies deep where the Marches meet
And the Northern wind is storming
When the powdery drift, drives fierce and swift
Filling hagg and syke and hollow
And Croziers' pack at the plantin' back
Are pairting wie' their tallow.

When ower the fell danders Croziers' sel'
And he looks baith dour and sulky
The sna's lain lang "and O! my sang"
The hay in the shed's no' bulky

Dark sorrow's trace has marked his face
Each day he's getting' thinner
He lang has ser'ed as a moorland herd
But he soon will be a skinner.

When up the hill marches roadman Bill
And faces these regions colder
With an action swift he tackles each drift
And heaves it o'er his shoulder
By his side there works these willing Turks
Brave Bod and Alexander
And that steam machine the famous Green
With a hiss like an angry gander.

With anxious eyes they view the skies
For a sign of the Western breezes
And then with a scowl and angry growl
Each gapes his gab and sneezes
They swing their arms till each cauld hand warms
And stamp their feet wie ire
Crying Oh! dear me for a cup o' tea
And a seat by the kitchen fire.

E'en Auld Nick himsel' on the Carter Fell
Wadna' stay in sic' stormy weather
We hae guid proof unless his hoof
Was held by a hempen tether
And its weel we ken that the smoky den
O' this famous brimstone charmer
Whate'er it be we can plainly see
Will indeed be a wee thought warmer.

Oh! its dour and snell on the Carter Fell
On a cauldrife winters morning
In that lone retreat where the Marches meet
And the Northern wind is storming
Its infernal cauld when ye're getting' auld
And ye're bluid is turning thinner
So ye're no' tae blame if ye stay at hame
As I'm a leevin' sinner.

LINES TO RAMBLER

We've seen ye come we've seen ye go
As years each other follow
We've seen ye scramble up each height
And ramble through each hollow.

Oh weel we ken ye love oor hills
Wie a' their wealth o' story
The witchery o' their wild romance
Has cast its glamour o'er ye.

Strang be your limbs then worthy Sir
Still stranger grow your muscle
And may ye lang be spared amang
The Cheviot Hills tae bustle.

Lang may ye wie auld herds convene
Tae cheer them at the clipping
We ken each morning ye yoursel'
Are handy at the "dipping".

And should ye hail some shepherds cot
Whist ye the streams are thrashing
Ye'll maybe gie the guid auld wife
A wee hand wie the washing.

And while upon the hempen line
The sna' white claes are drying
Ye'll jig the cradle wie yer tae
Whilst she some ham is frying.

But should the little wakefu' mite
Be fain tae raise a riot
Nae doot ye'll let it sook yer thoom
Tae keep the birkie quiet.

Thus prove yoursel a friend indeed
A kindly benefactor
Upon life's stage where every man
Fulfils his part as actor.

And when amang oor hills and dales
Nae langer ye can toddle
May many a pleasing thought o' them
Pass sweetly through yer noddle.

But oft in Redesdale classic glen
We hope for years tae see ye
So bid ye now Guid day auld frien'
And may aye joy gang wie ye.

347   *25 April 1933*

A FEARSOME DREAM

A month and mair I had been drinking
And ower the fire ae night sat blinking
When through my mind a vision passed
The wierdest Bacchus ever cast
Before me stood the strangest creature
That ever wore a human feature
Its frame was of immense proportions
And hideous looked as with contortions
It cast on me its withering glance
And round about did threatening prance
And frae its mouth whene'er it spoke
Came lowing flames and brimstone smoke
Its voice the air did rive asunder
More fearsome than a clap o' thunder
Its brow was large and seamed with scorn
And on it grew a crinkled horn
Its eyen like pots o' boiling lead
Deep sunken stared out of its head

Its teeth as black as Hareshaw coal
The hair a' singed frae off its poll
Its arms were ponderous and lang
Wie muscles knotted hard and strang
Its finger nails grew frae their sheath
Sharp lang and bent like Racker teeth
Its wame was big as Cheviot hill
And trackit ower wie mony a drill
Just like some field we may have seen
Where there'd a crap o' turnips been
Out o' its back a lang tail grow
But on't the hairs were thin and few
A knotty thing a' bent and twisted
As if it Time had lang resisted
Its legs o' length I will declare
Were ae Scotch mile or maybe mair
And of his feet ane was a club
Like an enormous washing tub
Nae wonder that my auld heart thumpit
And on my breast bane fairly duntit
And when it gat me in its grip
And me did 'neath its oxter slip
It needed nane the truth tae tell
I kenned it was the Deil himsel'
And off he bore me to these regions
Where dwell in torment Clootie's legions
While there I looked and feared and trembled
The hellish legions all assembled
While Nick cried out heat up the furness
We'll toast the chappie frae the Byrness.

An auld chiel in a grimy chocker
Stirred up the brimstone wie a pocker
Astonished sair I fairly gapit
And in a voice I kenned nae cheepit
I dinna doubt your power the least
But save us a' is that a priest
Auld Nick he notched and leugh wie scorn
And scratched his buttock wie his horn

Then winked and answered wie a leer
'Od man but I have a' kinds here
Just step this way and you shall see
If I am telling you a lee
He opened wide an iron door
My eyes saw ne'er the like before
There stood a Bishop in his apron
A Methodist wie pain was caperin'
A Plymoth rock wha's false delusion
Had landed him in sair confusion
A Roman Catholic wie his candles
Mahomaden wie feet in sandles
Presbyterians Covenanters
Salvationists blew loud their chanters
All creeds in fact frae every nation
To whom Auld Nick gave salutation
Come on my bonnie bairns he cried
I'm no' the loon to be defied
He spewed on them his brimstone reek
And puffed and blow out wide each cheek
While frae his eyes came lowin' darts
That pierced them tae their verra hearts
Their groans o' torment and o' pain
Resounder ower and ower again
While Nick seemed to enjoy himsel'
If there be any joy in Hell
He seized the pocker shank wie ire
And roosed anew the flaming fire
And just as shot up high the flame
An inspiration to me came
I pushed him in wie a' my might
And as he vanished oot o' sight
All Hell resounded with a scream
Which woke me from my awful dream.

TWELFTH PROSPECTS

I hollowed my nest on an April day
I cushioned my eggs where the bent grass lay
I kept them warm with my bosom heat
I turned them often with my tiny feet.
The clouds lay low on the misty fells
The day you stepped from your broken shells
I nursed you close as a mother should
For what my babes? Is the prospects good.

I led you by day in the shade of the ling
I closed you at night 'neath a covering wing
I broke you the path O my following ten
I taught you to flutter weak wings in the glen
I taught you to crouch from the hawks and hide
I bade you be brave when the curlew cried
I tugged at the heath to find you food
O babes of my heart, Is the prospects good.

Today they are busy in London town
Picking their guns for the journey down
Dreaming of smoke upon dark Ben More
And sitters leashed on Loch Steve shore
But who is there dreams of the days I spent
Making you wise in the fern and bent
Making you marked as the hills best brood
Babes little babes, Is the prospects good.

THE LAZY COUNTY ROADMEN

Who are the laziest men on earth
To whom good women ere gave birth

And Glendale with exultant mirth
  Yells just the County Roadmen.

Who bends their backs while spreading stones
Who oft has stiff and aching bones
Who is't emits mysterious groans
  The lazy County Roadmen.

Whose skin is blistered and whose eyes
Run water like the weeping skies
The men whom cold and heat defies
  The lazy County Roadmen.

When Boreas raves with drifting snow
Who o'er the trackless road doth go
And clears away the drifted snow
  The lazy County Roadmen.

Within the rural vale of Glen
Some Councillors discredit them
And class them as the laziest men
  The poor old County Roadmen.

They'd better come and have a day
At spreading stone at similar pay
They wouldn't have so much to say
  About the lazy Roadmen.

A pain they'd have in every joint
Their blistered hands they would anoint
Their muscles wracked at every point
  By working like the Roadmen.

Who made our grand Northumbrian roads
To carry such enormous loads
Why just the men whom Glendale goads
  Those idlers, The Roadmen.

5 Fred Terry's encounter with Billy Bell

Fred Terry was one of a famous theatrical family in Britain from late Victorian times. One sister was Ellen Terry, another was the grandmother of Sir John Gielgud, and his wife was a famous actress, Julia Neilson. Fred was an actor manager and his most famous role was Sir Percy Blakeney in The Scarlet Pimpernel, adapted from the novel by Baroness Orczy. He first played it in 1905 and toured extensively with it in the next twenty years. The article below was transcribed from Billy Bell's copy of the newspaper. One of the worst blizzards of the 20th century in the Borders was in February 1917.

ADVENTURES OF FAMOUS ACTOR AND ACTRESS
When Entertained at Wayside Cottage on the Borders

THE WEEKLY NEWS, SATURDAY, MARCH 3, 1917

(Written exclusively for the "Weekly News" by Fred. Terry.)

This is the first time that I have found an opportunity to relate the full story of the most remarkable experience - and suggestive of a modern touch of "The Scarlet Pimpernel" - that has ever befallen Miss Julia Neilson and myself, and which occurred a few days ago when we were "snowed up" on the Borders.

It was during our motor car journey from Newcastle to Aberdeen, or, to be precise, I should say our journey from Newcastle to the mountainous wilds of the Jedburgh district, for that is where we were blockaded by the snow.

It was at a humble cottage that my wife and myself received a welcome that proved easily the most cordial of our careers. Moreover I was given a compliment of a kind which I do not suppose it is often the privilege of any member of the theatrical profession to receive. But of that I will tell you later.

Let me give you what the present day matter-of-fact writers call a "plain, unvarnished story" of our adventures. The sun was shining from an almost, cloudless sky when we left Newcastle at half-post nine on that memorable Sunday morning. It was our intention to reach

Edinburgh in the evening, and then to press on to Aberdeen the following morning by rail or motor, according to the conditions.

Trouble.

The first sign of trouble in the shape of something flaky white appeared when we were about fifteen miles on the English side of Otterburn.

At first we thought it was just a small fall of snow, but, oh! dear no! It commenced to rattle against the car windows, and the sky became dark and ominous. We were constantly side slipping, and as we approached the mountainous country the chauffeur often found the utmost difficulty in controlling the car.

It was our hope to reach Jedburgh, where we could obtain lunch, for as the time went on we quickly disposed of what food we were carrying. The road was very narrow and there seemed to be high drifts of snow at each side so that often if we had decided to return it would have been a most dangerous thing to try and turn the car. We were now going at only a struggling pace.

Signs of life

With the appearance of the evening shadows on, I am sure, the stormiest day the district had experienced for years, Miss Julia Neilson uttered a sudden cry of joy - just as a wrecked mariner might do if he sighted a sail." Don't you see" she said, pointing over the brow of a snow-capped hill." There are two chimneys, and they are smoking. Surely here is warmth for us at last."

With eager expectancy we sprang to our feet and, peering through the window, we gradually saw what appeared to be two small cottages on the roadside. With the rustling and the groaning of the engine and the car only bumping along at a snail-like pace we ultimately reached these lonely places of habitation.

"And now," I said cheerily to my gallant comrades "our troubles are over, I feel sure, for a little time at all events."

I knocked at the door quite enthusiastically. It was opened by a middle-aged man, but I cannot say that I took any interest in that gentleman for the moment, for the opening of the door revealed to me a sight that made me smack my lips in anticipation of a good square meal, because hanging to the roof were 12 or 14 delicious looking hams. I put in a very modest request that seeing that we were "snowed up" we should be obliged with something to eat, even though we paid any price the owner liked to name.

Whether it was that the owner misunderstood or thought we were trying to play a practical joke you can imagine my astonishment when all the answer I got was this - "We have got plenty of mouths here for the hams."

I did not stop to parley or even investigate as to the reason for this strange reply, but decided to try my luck at the next cottage. How glad, too, I was that I did so, for we were becoming desperately in need of sustenance and warmth. In response to my knock a pleasant, kindly-faced woman appeared and I briefly explained to her our difficulty. She said her husband was away some miles distant helping to clear the snow from the road, and would be home soon, but in his absence she would do any thing she could for us

I asked her if she would let us sit in front of her fire. She agreed immediately and before many moments had elapsed the kettle, as the popular song goes, was singing on the hob and my wife was taking some nourishing cocoa, because she was rather distraught.

In the meantime Mrs Bell, our hostess, directed my chauffeur to a farm occupied by Mr and Mrs Nicholls, where she said he would be able to obtain plenty of eggs and other commodities of which she had not a very big supply, and certainly not sufficient for us, much as she was willing to provide us with all we needed.

My chauffeur found the way, and having been well received by the Nicholls, returned with eggs. Mrs Bell's cocoa and home- made bread had brought us back to a normal state of cheerfulness and I was relieved to hear that my chauffeur had been promised accommodation at the farm if necessary. And then Mr Bell returned, and a nicer man you could not meet.

He soon grasped the situation, and without wishing to unduly discourage us he told us plainly that we would never be able to get ahead until the snow had gone.

Worse Further On.

He had been a few miles up the road and there it was much worse. Most assuredly we could not do anything that night.

The only suggestion he could offer was that we should remain at his house that night, and then in the morning endeavour to get back again to Newcastle. He would go out first thing, and let us know what the conditions were like. And so we settled down in the fold of the Bells on this memorable Sunday evening. Mrs Bell prepared a bed for my wife, gave her hot water bottles, and after supper she retired and slept like the proverbial top. Now, owing to the limited accommodation at the Bells' rural home it was not possible for me to retire, so I decided to commandeer Mr Bell's armchair, sit before the fire, and snooze. That was alright, but Mr Bell would not hear of me sitting alone. "But," I said " my dear man, you've been up since five o'clock this morning; you will be too tired." Mr Bell, was quite firm, though, so we drew ourselves up to the cheery kitchen fire and sat and talked.

I enjoyed myself. Though the situation had looked very ugly, there was now something romantic about it all. And, oddly enough, just as in the story of "The Scarlet Pimpernel, a veil of mystery hung over my identity. I was like a Sir Percy Blakeney on a holiday. And unless Mr Bell reads these lines I do not suppose he will ever know who I happened to be.

But the story of the compliment – so sincere it was – is really good.

As the night wore on my host suddenly asked if I liked poetry. "Most certainly." I replied. "Well," says he, "I have done a little bit myself, and if you'd care to look at some of my lines I should be pleased.

"Delighted," I said, deeply interested.

And there in the dim light of an old fashioned oil lamp and the glimmering glow of a logged fire in that old, old cottage kitchen, where we were being entertained by two of the kindest hearts in the United Kingdom, I perused the writings of an undiscovered poet — a poet of the mountains, a man who looked upon Burns as his master, whom he worshipped from afar.

"These lines are really clever." I said enthusiastically.

"Would you do me a favour?" asked Mr Bell.

"Anything." I replied.

"Well, sir," he said, "will you please read my efforts aloud, for when anyone hears their writings read aloud they can observe their defects much better!"

A Compliment.

I read through all the verses, which touched various subjects — the hills, the houses, the winding lanes, the horses, and the cattle — and when I had finished Mr Bell looked at me with admiring eyes, and said. "You don't read badly."

"No?" I said. "I'm very glad to hear that."

I must admit that it required a little personal strain to conceal a smile, but having a fair experience, as I think you will agree, of portraying the apparently unconcerned demeanour of Sir Percy Blakeney, I succeeded in doing so.

Mr Bell, assisted by other workmen, later went along the road for several miles with their shovels, and as the snow had now ceased they were able to clear some parts of the road and also to make satisfactory report as to the chances of going south.

We embarked upon our way after breakfast, after paying sincere farewells to these good people. It was indeed really difficult to tell them the extent of our gratitude.

Billy Bell then wrote the story in verse

336

SNOWBOUND TRAVELLERS

From the good old town of Sunderland
Some travellers started forth
All seated in a motor car
They faced the magic North.

Full soon they left the Wear behind
And hailed the coaly Tyne
Whilst high o'erhead the sky was blue
And bright the sun did shine.

They struck the North West road and made
Out towards the rural scene
And soon they hoped to reach their goal
The town of Aberdeen.

But suddenly the sky grew grey
The snow began to fall
And o'er the landscape far and wide
Did spread its wintry pall.

With lightsome heart they journeyed on
No evil did they fear
Until they reached the mountains wild
So arctic and so drear.

Still fast and faster from the sky
Did fail the ermine snow
Which Boreas with his lusty breath
To mighty wreaths did blow.

Still slow and slower grow the pace
While stronger blew the blast
And often in the drifted snow
The motor ear stuck fast.

The cold did pierce them from without
Whilst hunger gnawed within
And oft they longed to find a place
And friend to take them in.

The Winter's day drew near its close
The shades of evening fell
But there seemed little chance of fire
Of food or an Hotel.

Until from lofty Saughenside
Two lonely cots they spied
And to seek shelter from the blast
These weary pilgrims tried.

Down from the lofty mountain top
They slowly made their way
With many a bump and many a jump
And many a fearsome sway.

At length outside these cottage doors
The motor car stood still
And forth assayed this hungry band
To forage with a will.

A cottage door thrown open wide
Increased their hungry qualms
As from the roof they saw displayed
One dozen bacon hams.

They made their plaint some food to buy
And any price to pay
Unmoved by hunger and distress
The inmates said them Nay.

Good breeding on the pilgrims part
But stayed their wild foray
Or else by force these hungry souls
Had borne these hams away.

With weary and with doleful looks
They left that cottage door
Yet pondered deeply why refused
From such abundant store.

Enquiries were further made
Our travellers were shocked
To know that further on the road
By snow was badly blocked.

To journey further Northward would
Have been a frantic feat
The gathering darkness too forbade
The chance of a retreat.

Then to my humble door they came
And made me this request
That I would spare them food and fire
And beds whereon to rest.

To this I gladly did consent
And took these strangers in
To have refused a dog a place
That night would have been a sin.

Soon on the hob the kettle sang
A merry merry tune
To them more sweet than Philomel
E'er sang through leafy June.

Then cheered with cocoa hot and strong
By Vulcan's ruddy hearth
Despair gave place to hopefulness
And woe gave place to mirth.

The evening meal at length was o'er
Sweet sleep its pleading pressed
Till only by the fire remained
The host and single guest.

We drew our chairs up to the glow
With faces all serene
Whilst burning incense at the Shrine
Of Lady Nicotine.

With conversation grave and gay
The passing minutes flew
It seemed as if old Father Time
Had oiled his wheels anew.

The kitchen clock prepared to strike
Its eerie midnight chimes
When I produced and showed my guest
My book of rustic rhymes.

He read my humble efforts o'er
I thought the action kind
I watched his face to try and catch
The workings of his mind.

At length he spoke his words were just
Encouraging sincere
They felt like nectar to my soul
And music to mine ear.

Emboldened by his kindly face I said,
"Sir would you read aloud?"
Most certainly, my guest replied
To do so I'll be proud.

My visitor at once complied
Indeed the truth to tell
He read my verses and I'll vow
He read them very well.

Unable longer to resist
The peaceful drowsy god
We said goodnight and took ourselves
Unto the land of Nod.

Next morning after break of day
We bade our guests adieu
They still were strangers unto us
As they are still to you.

A week went past a paper came
And in large print I read
Two famous actors snowed up
Fred Terry begs for bread.

I read the column to the end
Then gaily to my wife I cried
Come here old girl, our visitors
At last I have identified.

Oh who were they she quickly asked
And ceased from polishing the bars
Why bless my life, I cried good wife,
We've been amongst the "stars".

What! Stars? she said with, wondering eyes
And cheeks aglowing like a cherry
Stars of the great dramatic stage
Why Mr. Fred and Mrs. Terry.

Oh dear! she said we have been slow
Not to distinguish who they were
But never mind I'm very proud
We entertained the goodly pair.

Then let us sing long live the King
And Terry long live he
And when he next doth cross the Bar
May we be there to see.

6 Changing Conditions in Redesdale

Robert Craig - Written about 1936.

Although a few workmen's huts, stables and store-sheds were still awaiting demolition, the waterworks were completed, and the reservoir filled with water, when I came to Catcleugh. The young trees in the shelter-belts around the works, and in the rising plantations ranged from three to five years old. Consequently, the features of the landscape from a quarter of a mile below Catcleugh Farm up to the site of Lumsden had been materially changed. However, the social states of the upper reaches of the valley had once again returned to what may be termed a normal state.

Catcleugh, situated on a charming site, is in the Ecclesiatical Parish of Byrness, a mile and a half from the small church, in the Civil Parish of Elsdon [and] is four and a quarter miles from the Border Line at Carter Bar, six miles from Rochester, the nearest village and Post Office, and sixteen miles from the nearest railway stations. Woodburn S.E. and Jedburgh N.W., being equidistant. In 1910 facilities of travel to and from Catcleugh were very limited and expensive. The post-man's mail gigs were the cheapest mode of travelling up and down the valley, but the journey to, or from, Woodburn by that means took about four hours, and in winter was far from pleasant. Passengers changed gigs at Otterburn.

Notwithstanding that the solitary highway running through Upper Redesdale is one of the trunk roads leading into Scotland, there was very little through motor traffic on it in those days. In fact there was little through traffic of any description. It is quite safe to say that the members of the recently formed Catcleugh Angling Association, who came to fish on the reservoir, accounted for the major portion of motor traffic up and down Redesdale. The bulk of through traffic was composed chiefly of farm carts leading wool, feeding stuffs and artificial manure to and from the aforementioned railway stations, and an occasional traction-engine hauling a couple of waggons laden with the same class of materials. No doubt the hills and the rough state of the road surface were potent factors against travellers risking the Journey, especially in winter. Save for a few stretches at the head of

Redesdale, the road was not good. I may here say that the roads - the Main Road to Jedburgh and the Branch to Southdean and Hawick - on the Scottish side of Carter Bar, were in a deplorable state. It was not until about ten years after the Great War that any serious attempt was made to improve their condition. There is an old rhyme anent the roads in Upper Redesdale and over, the Carter which runs as follows:-

"Oh ye lands of hills and heather,
Stony roads and stormy weather:
Roads by people seldom trod
Roads entirely left to God."

While writing of roads it will be of interest to mention that only four permanent roadmen have been employed on the section from Carter Bar down to Byrness March, on Saughenside, since its reconstruction well over one hundred years ago. William Bell, the late roadman, who retired in April 1933 after a service of over fifty years, was formerly with the Upper Redesdale Road Board and latterly with the Northumberland County Council.

The busiest time of the year was for a week or ten days prior to, and a few days after, St. Boswells Fair, held annually on the 18th July, when companies of horse-dealers, hawkers, gypsies and kindred fraternity, with strings of horses, waggons and gaudy caravans, and divers types of horse-drawn vehicles, were trekking leisurely to and from the fair. "Yin's doorstep is never empty," was a common saying in the dale in those days, meaning that people living hard by the roadside, or within convenient walking distance of same, were pestered morning, noon and night, by relays of adults "boding" their wares for sale and wanting "handsel" in the mornings, children begging food and cast-off clothing, and picking up anything they could lay their hands on, and brazen-visaged, flammy-tongued females seeking to tell the fortunes of anyone whom they thought they could "gull". A field on the Scottish side of Carter Bar was favourite camping site but camping is now prohibited by the landowner. Another camping ground is at Bellshield about five miles down the valley from Catcleugh.

Not one of the carriers, provision merchants, general dealers and butchers from Jedburgh, Rochester, Otterburn, Elsdon and Woodburn, who supplied the inhabitants of Upper Redesdale with the commodities necessary for domestic needs, and the comforts of life, and who collected the produce of the; shepherds cows-and poultry, had a motor vehicle.

Now all is changed. To-day the horse-drawn vehicle, save the ordinary farm cart is a rarity and looked on as a novelty. With the introduction of the tar-binding system of road surfacing the roads have been greatly improved and through traffic has made a rapid advance. It has increased from units per week to hundreds in the winter and thousands in the summer. At the weekends there is a continual stream of motor traffic conveying hosts of sight-seers, pleasure-seekers, and no doubt, rest and health-seekers, up and down the valley. A case in point in regard to the first named craze, being in September, 1935 during the abnormal drought when the water level of the reservoir fell thirty-six feet. On the Sundays cars were parked along both sides of the road from Catcleugh to Lumsden. The merchants and tradesmen have all their own motor cars and motor vans and delivery waggons for transporting their goods. In the mad rush of competition tradesmen and commission salesmen travel long distances, to what was once called an "out-of-the-way place". A travelling shop comes periodically from Newcastle, and the people in Upper Redesdale can have a supply of fresh fish for breakfast every Tuesday morning, from Eyemouth. Our letters are now brought direct from Newcastle via Otterburn by a Royal Mail Motor van and are due to be delivered about 10.30. A.M.. Co-operation made its advent in Redesdale, when the Otterburn and District Co-operative Society was founded at Otterburn in March 1918.

In keeping with the changed and swifter means of travel and transport, old customs are dying out and are fast being superseded by new methods. The nomadic class, who at one time sought to linger by the way, now speed along in their motor cars. The glamour of the gaudy, expensive horse-drawn caravan and wayside camping under the bows of a waggon placed on the ground, is gradually fading out of the lives of that class. With the craze for speed a great majority of the annual frequenters of St.Boswells Fair travel up and down Redesdale by motor car and horse-dealers transport their horses in motor waggons. Many are equipped with modern trailers behind their motor cars, and only a small percentage of them hawk their merchandise en route.

159

Not so very long ago "droving" was an item of note on the shepherd's programme, and for some days prior to a special sale it was a regular sight to see shepherds in twos and threes driving large flocks of lambs or draft ewes along the main road, or over the drove roads on the hillsides to one or other of the sale centres. But with the great increase of motor traffic on the roads driving sheep or cattle has now become a difficult and dangerous business. The practice is dwindling yearly and is fast being superseded by motor transport. On the mornings of the special sales large double-deck motor waggons are a feature of the road traffic passing through the valley. I have seen draft ewes loaded at Catcleugh that were sold at Rothbury Auction Mart within two hours.

Although the chartered char-a-banc and motor 'bus conveying touring parties and trippers over requested routes gradually became a familiar sight, it was not until May 11th, 1928, that a regular motor 'bus service, through the valley was established. On that date, the Scottish Motor Traction Company commenced to run a service between Edinburgh and Newcastle via Jedburgh and Otterburn. On the following Monday a small Northumbrian company started to ply over the same route. These were shortly followed by the Clan Company whose 'buses plied between Glasgow and Newcastle, via Jedburgh and Otterburn. Sometime later the United Auto Services Ltd. came on. Eventually the P.M.T. and United took over the small companies and now jointly operate over the same routes. In winter there are two daily services each way. In summer these are augmented to four. I may here say that Mr Joseph Foster of Otterburn had previously established a service between Otterburn and Newcastle.

The coming of the motor 'bus services has been a boon to people living In Upper Redesdale and the Upper Reaches of Jedwater. The return fare to Newcastle from Catcleugh is less than one third of what a single motor car fare was from either Woodburn or Jedburgh stations, at the advent of the 'bus services. The journey of forty-one miles to Newcastle is done in about one hour and three-quarters. At the time of the Border, Glasgow and other Scottish holidays, and when troops from Scottish districts are being transported to and from Redesdale Artillery Camp at Birdhopecraig, a fleet of over a score of motor 'buses is a usual sight.

In 1912 Birdhopecraig Hall and farm together with the neighbouring farms lying on either side of the Sills Burn, on the Redesdale Estate and adjoining lands in Upper Coquetdale were bought by the War Office for the purpose of long range artillery practice. A Summer Camp with Birdhopecraig Hall for headquarters was established. With the exception of 1915-16-17-18, the years of the Great War the camp has been in regular use. In the Summer of 1918 *(?)* it was used as a prison camp for German prisoners. The camp provides employment for a good number of local men.

On the memorable Sunday night August 2nd, 1914 I took a young friend who was paying me a week-end visit down to see the camp. We were walking along the main thoroughfare when a bugler took up a position about forty yards from us, and sounded a call on his bugle. Instantly men were running from all directions, military police rushed down to the village and elsewhere to round up the stragglers. The men came in various guises, some in full uniform, some with only their breeches on and their boots unlaced, some in football costume and others in bathing dress, with their uniforms over their arms. The men lined up as they arrived and presented a rather motley sight. Briefly the Commanding Officer told them how the situation stood and what was expected of them. Again the bugle sounded and the men hurried to their respective posts. Soon all was hurry and bustle, overhauling guns and seeing that other equipment was in order and packing up in readiness to depart at a moment's notice should war be declared.

On March 14th, 1919, my friend again paid me a visit. He had been discharged from the Army of Occupation the previous week. We went down to Rochester on the Saturday afternoon, and as we passed the camp he remarked: "Little did I think when I heard the bugle sound the call for mobilisation that I would hear "cease fire" sounded on the battlefield."

State Forestry, although in its infancy in Upper Redesdale, is an industry that is destined to become an influential factor in the valley. The Forestry Commissioners took over Catcleugh from the Duke of Northumberland, and Byrness from the executors of the late Sir James Marr Bart, with the view of developing a State Forest in conjunction with the forest already under development at Kielder. Consequently the pastoral status of Upper Redesdale has been considerably reduced.

In September 1933, preparatory work, including surveying, draining and laying out turfs for planting on the Continental system of tree-planting and fencing was begun at the Byrness March on Saughenside. The enclosing and planting operations are carried out over an area of approximately five hundred acres, annually. In the summer of 1936, a small building scheme was begun and cottages were built at Byrness for the local members of the staff and other employees. With the development of the trees, the aspect of the district will gradually change, and in the course of time many interesting features of the landscape that can be seen from the road will be enshrouded from view.

In the spring of 1934, the Ministry of Labour, in furtherance their efforts in re-conditioning some of the unemployed in large industrial centres started a Summer Camp at Low Byrness. The camp accommodates staff and two hundred men. The period of their sojourn being three months. The work carried out by the trainees is road-making and bridge-building, and is being done in connection with the forestry scheme. In the summer of 1936 a substantial ferro-concrete bridge was built across the Rede below the confluence of the Cottonshope Burn. This piece of work is said to be the most important undertaking carried through by this class of labour.

7 Explore Billy Bell's home area

Base yourself in Tynedale or Redesdale in Northumberland. There are many hotels, B&Bs, self-catering cottages and caravan and camping sites. Tourist Information Centres have leaflets on the many attractions. Use the suggestions below for inspiration for whole or half days. Ordnance Survey maps will be useful.

1. Billy's grandfather came from and eventually settled back in the Irthing Valley near **Gilsland**. Billy's cousin Sallie helped her mother run a guesthouse at Dacre House in Gilsland. Like those visitors explore the Irthing Valley and **Birdoswald** Roman Fort.

2. **Hexham** is where Billy would have watched the circus described in the "Woodburn Cylists" poem (83). Spend some time exploring the town, the **Old Gaol**, the **Abbey** and the riverside.

3. **Bellingham** is the setting for three poems about Bellingham Show and is where births, marriages and deaths for Billy's family were registered. Walk up to the waterfall at **Hareshaw Lynn** and visit the **Heritage Centre** based in the old railway station.

4. Billy's father moved from Simonburn to work on a farm at Plashetts, now under **Kielder Water**, the reservoir that in 1981 flooded parts of the old Border Counties Railway which Billy travelled on as a newly born infant just after it opened.

5. His father and uncles were born at Halton near to **Corbridge** which has inns, cafes and interesting shops as well as good local walks. Visit **Aydon Castle** and **Corstopitum** Roman Fort.

6. Sweep north up the A68 from Corbridge - watching out for blind dips in the road. Spot the "castle" at **West Woodburn** that was actually part of the 19th century iron works (and has fooled several experts). Continue up to **Byrness** where Billy lived.

Visit the church and churchyard. At the south end of Catcleugh Reservoir walk along the road that tops the dam wall. Drive north alongside **Catcleugh Reservoir** to Carter Bar. The A68 from Rochester to Carter Bar, was Billy's stretch of road.

7. Cross the Border at **Carter Bar** on the A68 to go to **Jedburgh**. Walk up Castlegate where his mother lived and visit Jedburgh Abbey. Continue on to **Kelso**. Visit **Floors Castle** where his mother worked as a house servant for a few years.

8. South of Byrness, visit **Bremenium Fort** at High Rochester, just off the A68; go south to Otterburn and look out for **Shittleheugh Bastle** (his brother worked at the farm there). After you have explored **Otterburn** (which is where Billy met his first wife, Mary) continue south and turn off to **Elsdon**. This is where Mary was born. In 1866 George Chatt wrote a poem denigrating Elsdon as "the world's unfinished neuk". Fifty years later Billy wrote a riposte praising the village and its inhabitants. Find the pub Billy called the 'Blackbirds Nest'.

9. Continue across the hills from Elsdon to the **Coquet Valley**. Imagine life as a shepherd in these hills. Explore up the valley towards Alwinton or follow the valley down to **Rothbury**. While you are there go to **Cragside** - the first private house in the world lit by electricity.

10. For a longer trip go to **Alnwick**. Visit the **Castle** and the **Gardens**. Barter Books is located in the old Railway Station.

If, after this, you want an excuse to visit somewhere more urban then Billy wrote to, and visited, his nephews and nieces at Willington on Tyneside. **Tynemouth Castle and Priory** and **Seaton Delaval Hall** are nearby on the coast. The largest shopping areas are **Newcastle city centre** and the **Metrocentre** on the Gateshead side of the Tyne.

Poem Index - Alphabetical